Ignore the Paradigm Shift; at your peril

```
I0390693
```

Old Style Sales and Marketing

Rules have Changed
How do you get information?
Where you look up answers to trivia?
Do you open an encyclopedia to pull up information on history?
Do you still get a Yellow Pages delivered to look up a phone number?
Selling Expertise and Effectiveness IS the problem.

Some information is used multiple places, because as an entrepreneur …you've probably already started to skim, and all these tools are interconnected.

Eight reasons digital communication changed the world (use them)

One: **Many people and locations can connect and communicate at the same time**. Every voice involved in a discussion can engage simultaneously without meeting in the same physical location. Group emails, webcast, and video conferencing (all free) allow all participants to speak face-to-face (screen-to-screen), edit documents, and even sign legal contracts from any computer—anywhere in the world... drop the Mic!

Two: **24/7 availability to address and respond to a question.** We engage a topic when we choose. This leisure of communication means that others answer us when they want to as well. Selfish pressing of a potential client to give you their business on your timeline will typically push them away. Old sales tricks involved timing (when to interrupt a conversation), or stopping in the office at five o'clock to get a contract signature (once the secretary had left for the day). Now, if you send me an email with a contract attachment; I will respond when it is best for me to address it. If I review the contract at 2am, I can set my email to be delivered in the morning (so I don't seem desperate by working at 2am). I can also send a team update email at 2:05am that's written at 4:20pm to appear to be the most industrious person in the company. We control our timing.

Three: **Confirm accuracy and expertise before giving a response.** If you don't know the answer, you don't have to respond immediately. Look it up. Find an expert who knows more than you on the topic (even if that expert is an internet search). Confirm the right answer so that when you do respond it is a verified fact—rather than your best guess. The person waiting for your answer doesn't have to know whether you were delayed due to an unexpected phone call, or if you were researching the question. The client's experience is; you were the expert that provided the insight they can trust with their next need.

Four: Communicate a complete response without interruption.
Few conversations are more annoying than those that involve someone asking for information who won't shut up long enough to listen to the answer. Electronic communication allows deliberate intentionality—up to the point it is sent. Easily share paperwork, illustrations, client endorsements, or almost anything you desire in validating your point and perspective; positioning you as the right expert to trust.

Five: Ignore unwanted advances without a "break-up" talk.
At times polite engagement is interpreted as an open door to pushy sales. On behalf of all sales people... I'm sorry. Overly aggressive sales people usually lack the conversational skills that include "appropriate" awareness. This resolution is becoming a cliché; unwanted advances can be filtered to a junk mail folder... permanently (without ever needing to address the offending party) ... so be careful to not annoy.

Six: Keep a written record of every step in the sales cycle.
Unfulfilled expectations can't be ignored. Separating actual promises made from unspoken expectations offers clarity and freedom. When a customer complaint arises (it happens to all of us) - our communication history will clearly expose the depth of compromise that you will offer in satisfying the customer. A simple email chain can record every step in the negotiation process... if you record every step of the sales process with confirmation emails.

Seven: Abrupt changes in the trajectory of the conversation are simple and direct and identifiable.

There is no longer an uncomfortable group silence when you give "no" for an answer. If a new vendor or partner joins the negotiation; simply forward the pertinent emails. All parties involved are caught up with minimal investment of time. This system carries an intrinsic security against a "biased rewording of the current status" (an old school sales trick that needs exterminated).

Eight: You don't have to think quick to reply with wisdom.

I wish more people took advantage of this feature. Allowing emotions to subside before responding to an offensive statement is always better than a heartfelt apology afterward. When you are provoked, don't answer immediately. Watch a video of your children, go for a walk, or do whatever alters the chemicals racing through your system that create the confrontational emotional feeling—and manipulate yourself into a better mood. Once you are chemically balanced... then return and reply with wisdom. Through this entire process, you never leave the conversation - you just leave your self-sabotaging actions and words in the realm of "might have been".

The Problem with Sales & Marketing in a Digital Age

The internet is baffling to sales and marketing, because the tools don't directly line up with the traditional process.

Top marketing minds;

>   (1) understand the message,

>   (2) target an audience, and

>   (3) design a campaign.

Great sales people;

>   (1) professionally locate a prospect,

>   (2) categorize and follow up leads, and

>   (3) close when the timing is right.

Both of these finish with step (4) analyze and adjust for effectiveness.

The digital world has developed so fluidly that tool names and categories aren't established; much less having a standardized system for how to use them (or where they fit daily tasks).

Traditional tools established the traditional sales cycle. The only sales and marketing choices were how much to invest in each tool to create the desired end result. Many of these tools still exist (and work if the industry is still around).

- *Traditional Tools: Trade Shows, Newspapers, Billboards, Business Cards, Newsletters, Flyers, Telemarketing, Display Booths, Phone Calls, Cold Calling, Junk Mail, TV & Radio Ads, Classifieds, Bulletin Boards, Yellow Pages, Storefront, and sometimes Referrals.*

Digital tools can be used in any step of the sales and marketing process (some require use in all the steps). Success of a campaign is based on the **proper selection of which tools your <u>target client</u> is using and sequencing the tools used to appear as natural as a face to face conversation**, because THE TARGET is the person that you are trying to reach. The order with which these pieces are created is essential, but the process in which they are engaged (by the client) is largely unpredictable.

- *Digital Tools: Websites, Social Networks, Domains, Hosting, Directories, Social Media, Email, Text, SEO, SEM, PPC, Analytics, Forums, Groups, Blogging, Message Signatures, Response Forms, Landing Pages, Check-ins, Endorsements, Videos, Podcasts, Webinars, Cloud Backup, E-commerce, Keywords, and maybe someday Sales.*

Use the right tool at the right time for an intentional end result.

Where do we go from here?

The web can extend your reach, or destroy your aim. A clear plan and process is necessary and will keep you from spinning your wheels with pointless activity and this guide is designed to protect you from frustration. Behavioral sales and marketing tools are simple, but vital in order to thrive in today's socially digital age.

Old School errors that will handicap your efforts?

- Pushy sales funnel, traditional cold calling, tricking gatekeepers, and the ability for the big guys to have an "in" that you don't.

What do the tools of the digital age offer?

- Easy and effective calls-to-action, mutually beneficial sales process (to put the client at ease rather than manipulate them to your own end), and use your computer to do much of the automated busy work a personal secretary used to do.

Our culture grows out of centuries of communication so we don't have to start over from the beginning each time we take on a new task. Our communication allows us to use other people's past successes and failures. Behavioral sales and marketing in the digital age will allow you to engage people you enjoy. Some of those relationships will turn into referring new clients that will expand your business.

****

Congratulations,

You're taking the leap

into the new paradigm.

It's moving...

with or without you, so...

Welcome.

Table of Contents

Start here... who are you?

I like to think of myself as a vast combination of unique factors that have made me what I am today; and I prefer to view those around me with general assumptions that are based on the choices they have made. I have reasons for my actions; they have excuses. The most effective brands honestly assess themselves and others.

Sales & marketing starts with understanding how we are seen.
- General assumptions are real (whether they're justified or not)
- We choose to be and do

The client is a Vast combination of unique factors that have made them what they are

Knowing yourself is the launch pad that must be secure before you can ever create a brand to orbit above your pitch (which is business).

Reality doesn't matter - **perception** is reality

In order to understand others, it is vital that you
- **Admit** who you are
- **Know** what you believe
- **Choose** what you focus on
- **Change** or **enhance** whatever mental framework you are in

Learn the processes by which you create the internal movie of the outside reality.

Our subjective experience has a structure, and how we think about something affects how we experience it.

In almost every communication, we can be sure
- What we **say** is rarely (if ever) what is **received**
- What we **understand** is almost never exactly what is being **communicated**

You cannot - not communicate.
- **70% of communication is non-verbal**
- **Silence can communicate more powerfully than words could ever attain.**

What do others see as 'you'?

Past experiences
Present communication
Expressions of Future expectations

Know Yourself to Read Others

True self-assessment is painful. It is intrusively exposing in areas that we have (likely) given great effort to cover. A raw view of yourself and assessing what is strong and weak creates the potential that (every once in a while) you may need to put the book down and get yourself a cup of coffee or something stronger to drink. If it's painful to truly assess yourself. You can know that you are doing the hard work when you find yourself at the end of your resources in a certain area. As with anything of worth, you do the hard work on the front end or on the backend. The longer you wait—the higher the cost when you get around to doing what you have avoided.

How you are viewed comes complete with general assumptions and information filters; all mixed up with experiences that potential clients have had in the past. How you envision yourself is not always in line with the opinions held by the person across the table.

The digital sun rises and sets on **personal brand.**

We like to think of ourselves as a vast and glorious combination of the unforeseeable factors that are unique to our life experience. We justify this perspective with optimistic recollection of the "tough circumstances" that have influenced our path - all of which have made us into who we are. Yet, while we optimistically frame these translations of our past, we pessimistically frame the translations of other's past (even those with the exact same historical circumstances as us). As with most points of reality, truth is more universal than our minutely selfish view allows.

It is beneficial to see *the client* as a vast combination of unique factors that have made them who they are - **because that is how the client sees themselves**. This way you're both working from the same viewpoint.

You're not there to fix your client—you're there to do business. You're there to sell.

We only ever influence the areas that we are given permission to affect. You have permission to do business - stick to that for now. **Reality doesn't matter—only your client's perception of reality**. How they perceive you *is* their reality. Your abilities to process who they are (their weaknesses and strengths) are nothing more than tools in your arsenal that help you understand... what *is*. Figure out who they are and how they see you in order to move forward with business.

In order to understand others, you must admit who you are. Know what you believe. Choose what you focus on. Change or enhance (when necessary) whatever state you are in. Learn the process by which the internal movie of your outside reality is created, and **focus on the only part of that internal screenplay that you are truly in control of... yourself.**

If your internal or external dialog leading up to an appointment is, "This person is a pain in the butt", or "I don't want to deal with them" or "I can't believe that they don't do [this or that] to make it better"... you're polluting the conversation with outside factors that have nothing to do with your purpose. These pollutants will do nothing besides cloud your mind. Simplify; adjust your focus to their perspective and you can engage them **as they are**. This creates one variable (the customer), rather than two.

You will be the one in control, because you're the one who is flexible and free to

engage them as they really are (even when they can't see themselves).

We often deceive ourselves when dealing with difficult (or even loved) people because;

we assume *they* will change once we share what we have in our mind—because *they* would see things just like us if *they* could only understand what we know.

The solution to this puzzle is to have a firm grasp on yourself, because self is the only piece that you truly have control over. This is the soil your Brand grows out of.

For Instance: Target Perspective Assessment of my Brand

Even as I read this; I catch myself thinking of specific people who need to change. How do I handle people who demand my attention, and yet all that I struggle with is based on *their* words and *their* actions (and *their* brokenness I don't have permission to fix)?

- How does their understanding of my past experiences draw and/or repel that individual?

- What am I trying to fix or grow or ignore in that person (is it business or personal)?

- If nothing ever changes—will my life be better to struggle, compromise, or give in?

Test Questions: *(sometimes making it a game, makes it easier)*

- ***Walk through each trouble client and ask:***
  - ***What is my purpose in engaging him or her?***
  - ***What is in my control to make it more fun?***

Always give Value

Buyers believe they can <u>get</u> what you <u>sell</u> from a number of other vendors
- Accuracy of their opinion doesn't matter
- If the buyer thinks it - it's a reality in the *only mind that matters*
- Reality of the Marketplace: whatever you sell <u>is a commodity</u>

FAB is dead (<u>F</u>eature <u>A</u>dvantage <u>B</u>enefit) and resurrected as VALUE
- If you are aiming at setting yourself apart based on Feature, Advantage, and Benefit the only way to consistently earn business is <u>Lower</u> your <u>Price</u>
- This is unsustainable in today's "economy of scale" based business world - because there's always someone bigger (and cheaper)

Opportunity comes from the market place lacking <u>product differentiation</u>
- People place high value on useful advice
- Corporate Experts are the second most valued opinion (next to academic experts)

THE VALUE HOOK:
- If you consistently create content that shows your expertise, buyers will look for you when they're in the market
- Does giving up your expertise overrides the benefit of changing vendors - even at a lower price

---

Buyers are currently <u>online</u> looking for value

- We search online for information to figure out the best option (for ourselves)

- Buyers want your sales pitch to be available when they're looking for it, but not pushed upon them

Your Brand is whatever *they* think it is

Harness your Superpower of Assumptions and Expectations - we have more power than we think.

It is wise to assess past obstacles. It is foolish to trap my imagination into a cycling-view of negative scenarios that only feed on my emotional reaction. It may feel good growing my addiction to [whatever appetite/emotion being fed], but it is typically not beneficial to a new client signing the contract. Control of self will supercharge any communicator, and a good brand will become the frame.

For Instance: What's in your Focus?

Studies on memory and intelligence in an aging population suggest that the more you think about losing your memory—the better chance you have of losing your memory. The more you use your memory in your engagement of daily life... the longer it lasts.

If you focus on the problem, it only gets bigger. Focus the solutions, and the problem diminishes. We don't have time to focus on all the problems, or we'd have to set up therapy sessions for decades to come. In solution focused therapy (for example) the proof shows that when you focus on a problem... the problem gets bigger. When you focus on the solution... the solution grows.

We deplete our own resources to fight against the very thing we are battling to kill. Irony seems cruel when you oppose the natural order of things.

Giving effort to overcome past issues is a worthy endeavor. Pretending that there is nothing wrong

is senseless!

Annoying circumstances, destructive problems, and reoccurring difficulties are real, however they should never be the default point of focus (at least not for too long). **In a fascinating twist of** interpersonal physics, the energy source for that fear or habit—becomes you.

- Aristotle (the Greek philosopher) said, *"A good character carries with it the highest power of causing a thing to be believed."*

- Jesus (the founder of the world's largest religion) said, *"The power of life and death are in the tongue."*

A Game: What's in your Focus?

If you consider yourself to be shy, take eight minutes to imagine the best case scenario *if you were socially confident*. Close your eyes and See and Hear yourself in confident conversations. Allow your imagination to play through social interactions with enough detail to mentally and emotionally experience what you desire your current reality to reflect.

Your beliefs may need to get past your memories.

If you're trying to adjust a habitual occurrence; the more vividly you can see yourself in a 'character' that is not historically what you have presented or acted out, the quicker you will enable yourself to be… whomever you have imagined yourself to be.

Make sure your Brand is in line with whomever you want to become.

Why build personal brand?

The purpose of your personal brand is to balance Trust vs. Risk (in the client's mind).

Trust vs. Risk

- People get <u>advice</u> from any expert they find, but they <u>buy</u> from brands they trust
  - o If they don't know you, they'll typically buy from a brand that their friends refer
  - o The more familiar you are with the prospective buyer, the less perception of risk in doing business with you

- <u>Trust</u> is what draws prospects to you

- <u>Risk</u> is what pulls prospects away from you

- Recommendations to your personal brand can come in the form of:
  - o Letter of Recommendation
  - o Review on a Directory (Google, Yelp, Yahoo)
    - with any review, start with getting a few "five star reviews".
      - Go to business.google.com, facebook.com, yelp.com; look up your business
      - If you don't show up (bigger deal than getting a review)
    - It's easier to compensate for a 2-3 star review when you have a few 5 stars first
  - o Endorsements on Social Media
    - Positive Tweets should be marked as "favorite" (click the star)

What is your Brand?
- You don't have to create an entirely new product to establish a unique personal brand

- What's your <u>Unique Value Proposition</u>?
  - o Use one characteristic to distinguish yourself online
  - o What is it that makes you <u>stand out</u>?

TOMATO: is a great guide for modern branding

- <u>T</u> op
- <u>O</u> f
- <u>M</u> ind
- <u>A</u> wareness
- <u>T</u> hrough
- <u>O</u> thers

Form a Target Client Focused Brand

Consumers collect advice from any expert that sounds reputable, but we purchase from those we trust. If we don't know anyone in a certain field, we'll buy from people that our friends (or trusted sources) validate as safe - by referral. **Upside potential to downside risk is the calculation that determines your brand's likelihood of referral.**

Get positive endorsements on every channel you know. Each time someone likes your company page/profile/etc; it tells *their network* that your company is a safe business. If someone sends you a message that sings your praise on Google/Yelp/Facebook, save it as a favorite/bookmark/etc. so that visitors can find them. An old management cliché is to criticize is private and praise in public. If someone offers you a praise - make it public.

Be a Happy Brand - it's attractive!

It is not necessary to wait for a kind word to spontaneously appear. It is acceptable (and wise) to ask for referrals. Each time someone gives you a complement - immediately ask them if they'd be willing to say that on social media or a directory listing. Whatever conversation you have on social media should always be in the positive (at least as it is within your control).

What is your brand? You don't have to create an entirely new product to establish a unique personal brand.

- Use <u>one characteristic</u> to distinguish yourself (clients typically remember only one).
- Write out the <u>unique value proposition</u> of your Brand;
  - Something that makes you standout
  - Something that makes you exceptional
  - A point, a thought, a concept, that *in your industry*, you might be the only one who sees what you see.

Referrals are the rain making source of sales today, and your business lifeblood tomorrow. Give them a reason to refer.

The Six Scripts

There are a few personalized tools that every sales and/or marketing business person must have. <u>Create them now</u>.

<u>The Six Scripts:</u>

1. <u>Headline:</u> This is a phrase that is no more than 140 characters and is "The One Thing", but remember that LESS IS MORE.

2. <u>Unique Value Pitch:</u> People buy value; sell it with a statement.

3. <u>Elevator Pitch</u>: answer to the "so, what do you do?" question. It's called an elevator pitch because it's able to be given in the time of an elevator ride (leaving time to hear their elevator pitch too).

4. <u>Appointment Offer</u>: A two-minute reason why your target client should meet with you.

5. <u>Your Story</u>: Answer to how/why did you get into that field?

6. <u>Biography</u>: Name dropping synopsis of your expertise.

Define: Buying Cycle, Pipeline, and Pitch

- <u>Pitch or Ask</u>: Question that (when answered) closes the negotiation.

- <u>Buying Cycle</u>: The cycle of; marketing to sale to referral (that almost all business communication follows).

  - This is the normal cycle of business. Recognize; the client only focuses on this buying cycle once in a while (so continual hand holding is likely needed and productive).

- <u>Pipeline</u>: The process of tracking one company or individual through the buying cycle; ensuring that no one is lost or allowed to continue too far.

Sales Tip: Sales is Acting

Business and sales in everyday life is really nothing more than acting. You have your role, you have your script, and the better you communicate your lines and the more you engage your role, the better you do.

<u>Create them</u>

<u>now.</u>

1. Headline

- This is a simple statement that is shorter than the elevator pitch, but captures as much of your essence that only fewer words are capable of doing.
- Imagine the headline as the:
  - Newspaper front page article that you would like to see on tomorrow's paper
  - A Billboard that will be directly out front for everyone that comes to your office to read
  - This is the Elevator Pitch - reduced
- Play with this and tweak it until it's exactly what you want
  - However, it reads, everyone in your business should know this and recite it without thinking

(word game):

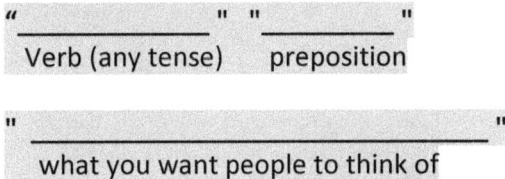

"_____" "_____"
Verb (any tense)   preposition

"_____"
what you want people to think of

Define: What are the Different Parts of Speech?

- A noun is a word describing a person, place, or thing.
- An adjective is a word or phrase naming an attribute to describe or modify that noun.
- A verb is a word used to describe an action, state or occurrence.
- An adverb is a word or phrase describing a verb (or another adverb).
- A pronoun is a short/general word used in the place of a noun (he, she, it, they...)
- The most common Prepositions are: about, above, across, after, against, along, among, around, at, before, behind, below, beneath, beside, between, beyond, but, by, despite, down, during, except, for, from, in, inside, into, like, near, of, off, on, onto, out, outside, over, past, since, through, throughout, till, to, toward, under, underneath, until, up, upon, with, within, and without.

2. Unique Value Pitch (sample script in gray)

(word game):

"_____ brings value to "
      Business Name

"_____ "
   Target client plural generalization (job title, industry niche, etc)

"_____ "
Preposition

(Transferable section)

"_____ "
  Adjective ending in "ly"

"_____ "
  Verb ending with "ing" (describing solution)

" the_____ , so "
Client's slang to generalize this product/service/industry (humor is best)

"_____ is/are "
  Short (Noun/Adjective) description of the core pain being resolved

(headline)

"_____ " "_____ "
   verb   preposition

"_____ "
  what you want people to think of

- **Business to Business** - Joe's Barbers brings value to local executives through endlessly perfecting the sad state of barber options, so classy executives are groomed to perfection.
- **Retail** - Sally's Café brings value to our neighborhood through deliciously saving the same old chicken dinner so saving money on better food is heated with love.
- **Consultant/proprietor** - Tibbs Insurance brings value to small business owners with consistently reviewing the BS government regulations around real estate, so unexpected bills are covered in trust.

3. Elevator pitch

- The elevator pitch should be able to be given in 10 seconds or less and is the answer to the question, "what do you do?"
- It is stated/written as a complete thought and gives in the simplest, most straight forward format the big picture of what you are about
- As you fill out the Pitch Template,
  - Select the top words that describe who you are and what you do/what makes you unique to the client/prospect
  - After you have the words you want to use, you need to write out the "Elevator Pitch"
    - Make it clear
    - Make it easy to memorize and say
    - Make it sound like you
    - Make it describe your business so people will understand the core of who you are
    (use as few words as possible)

Elevator Pitch:
Denver CenterPoint is a Family of Employees incubating businesses through on site Ownership, Management and Leasing that Redefines Responsive Professionalism.

- There are also opportunities (mostly online) that you can give a longer elevator pitch that will be read. These "Longer Elevator Pitches" are good places to stuff keywords
- Don't "keyword stuff" social profiles! Make them readable; because if your info is not readable, the network will likely blacklist you (and no one will be able to find you - even when they're looking)

LONGER KEYWORD HEAVY DESCRIPTION:
Whether you are looking for **offices in Denver, suites in Denver** or simply to **address virtually,** Denver CenterPoint 1 has something for you. With **ample conference room space** and **views of the entire range** of Denver's **Rocky Mountains,** there is no place more **central,** attractive or legitimately wise for your **commercial real estate** presence.

- There are still other situations online that will allow both the Elevator Pitch and the longer keyword heavy elevator pitch to be used together. Since you don't want to retype both of these each time you come across this situation, it's good to combine them and have them available in a digital format for copy and paste functionality later.

Both:

Denver CenterPoint is a Family of Employees incubating businesses through on site Ownership, Management and Leasing that Redefines Responsive Professionalism. Whether you are looking for offices in Denver, suites in Denver or simply to address virtually, Denver CenterPoint 1 has something for you. With ample conference room space and views of the entire range of Denver's Rocky Mountains, there is no place more central, attractive or legitimately wise for your commercial real estate presence.

*** Elevator Pitch (word game): ***

1. Your Name: " _____ is/are"
   - Business to Business   - *ABC Offices*
   - Retail   - *XYZ Barbers*
   - Consultant/proprietor - *John Doe*

2. Define business structure (noun with adjective):
   " _____ "
   - Business to Business   - *a Family of Employees*
   - Retail   - *the top professionals*
   - Consultant/proprietor - *the Insurance Expert*

3. Action (verb) that hints at what sets you apart:
   " _____ "
   - Business to Business   - *custom fitting*
   - Retail   - *leading*
   - Consultant/proprietor - *uncovering*

4. Your Product or Service being provided: " _____ "
   - Business to Business   - *business office space*
   - Retail   - *men's grooming expertise*
   - Consultant/proprietor - *affordable liability coverage*

5. Prepositional Phrase: " _____ "
   - Business to Business   - *through*
   - Retail   - *to*
   - Consultant/proprietor - *with*

6. Unique Value Pitch: (previous script)

4. Appointment Offer

A request to meet for a pitch appointment has more to do with a personal connection as the pitch itself. Every product and service, business and sales person needs their own customized version of this. This two-minute pitch adds meat to the bones of the Elevator Pitch. There are a couple points of consideration required to make this tool really work:

1. Inspire with your emotional buy-in to what you are pitching (emotion sells).

2. After expounding on why each piece of the Elevator pitch is necessary, **end with a clear and specific offer to meet to discuss what you offer (THAT OFFER IS THIS SCRIPT).**

The best way to create this "Appointment Offer" is to use it as the ending to "Your Story" (next), and write it out.

Once you have it written out, pick a couple family members, friends, colleagues and clients to say it to verbally. *This is painful and you will want to skip this step.*

If you are comfortable giving this appointment offer to those four categories of contacts, you will be comfortable enough to start trying it on people you meet.

We have a tendency to be willing to screw up pitches to strangers, but embarrassed when messing up communication with people we like or respect. Those strangers are our paychecks of tomorrow.

Get your pitch right and use it to increase your worth.

Sales Tip: Silence Power

There comes a point in every ask/pitch when the question has been presented and the only next step is an answer. This is when many sales people ruin the whole thing. Please stand there; look them in the eye and wait... it is only uncomfortable the first few times you shut up & listen... and then it becomes kind of fun. **Don't sell past the close!** Ask... and... keep quiet!

Sales Tip: Alternative Choice Close (good with Appointment Setting)

There are countless types of 'closing techniques'. One of the most common (and effective) is the Alternative Choice Close. There is rarely a time that a pitch should be able to be answered with a "Yes" or "No". This is fixed by offering alternative choices in your questions.

The simple example is, "would you like it in <u>blue</u> _or_ <u>green</u>". Current psychological study says that 3 choices are best... I disagree with that. If you narrow it down to two choices, then there can be one issue that you're solving. Priority is required.

It's easy to become sloppy on appointment requests, because we know that our schedule could be open to meet at any time with someone who is going to give us a large sum of money (which is the same as a large sale). Because of this—we sound too available... even desperate.

My favorite ask, "Is there a time of day or day of the week that works best for you?" If that doesn't create an option, pick a morning next Tuesday and an afternoon 2 Thursdays away. You need sales then too—start building your pipeline.

5. Your Story

"How did you find your way into that line of work?"

"Your Story" is about your business, but spoken in the narrative of your professional journey.
Facts are beneficial benchmarks, but not what people are interested in when they ask for your story. The points they recall when remembering their story are based on the pains, frustrations, accomplishments and joys in their rear view mirrors. Even when we aren't completely proud of our current position, the steps and experiences that brought us here create how we see ourselves, and that is exactly how we want others to see us.

Questions to help build Your Story:
- **What was your most educational relationship?**
- **What is your favorite accomplishment?**
- **How will the fulfillment of your business mission and vision benefit your clients?**
- **What is the most inspiring story you have about yourself?**
- **This doesn't have to be about your business, just tied in to your Unique Value Proposition.**
- **Describe the business deal that provided the greatest benefit to a client.**
- **What benevolent activities or deals expose your commitment to the great good of our society?**

A "Your Story" is about who you are and what has made you that way. Due to the personal nature of a "Your Story" it is just as important *how* you say it as *what* you say. If you're someone who has difficulties adding intentional emotion to prepared and written statements, there are countless acting coaches that are waiting to be hired to help you (this acting job is your only job - get good).

It's beneficial to remember that (even though you are telling "Your Story" in an emotionally provocative manner) your intent is to be understood, and set yourself up to fully understand their story. **The sales process is not about you, it's always about them.**

- Through all these tools, you are trying to understand:
  - Who they are
  - What they do
  - How they do it
  - When they need help
  - Why you can help them

Purpose & Vision: You should be able to articulate these and fit them into "Your Story", no matter what your position in the company is.

- What is your mission?
- **What benefits do we want your customer to get from our organization?**
- Who is our main customer?
- *How do we gauge they are getting these benefits?*

Your Story... defined

Purpose & Vision: these are points that you should be able to articulate, even if you aren't the owner of the company.

- <u>What is your mission?</u>_____
  _____

  _____

- <u>Who is our customer?</u>_____
  _____

  _____

- <u>What benefits do we want your customer to get from our organization?</u>_____
  _____

  _____

- <u>How do we know if they are getting these benefits?</u>

  _____

- *Write the answer to the question, "How did you find your way into that line of work?"*

  _____

  _____

- A 'Your Story" should have to do with your business, but be told in the narrative of your professional journey.
  - o Facts are not what people are interested in when they ask for your story

  _____

- Facts are not what people are telling you when they give you their story

  _____

  - They want you to see them for who they really are.
    - Successful (based on their circumstances)
    - Able (if given the right opportunities)
    - Kind (inside, even if situations don't expose their best attributes)
  - A "Your Story" is about who a person is and what has made you/them that way
    - Treat is as such; be creative

- Write an outline of how "Your Story" should be told
  - Write it out for details and then learn it to express emotions
  - It's important to remember that (even though you are telling "Your Story" in an emotionally provocative manner) your intent is to understand their story.
  - It's not about you, it's always about them
  - You are just trying to understand
    - Who they are
    - What they do
    - How they do it
    - When they need help
    - How you can help them

After writing out "Your Story" it's a good idea to create a series of images to help you memorize the main points and tell it the same way every time so you know what people have heard and you don't get repetitive.

- *The lead/client is allowed to repeat themselves, you are not; unless it's on purpose.*

6. Biography

A good biography (bio) in today's social media world is required. Just about every social network, directory, and website has a place for your bio. A primary purpose for creating a solid biography is that some potential clients will look to do business with you based on this tool.

- Give the highlights of your career
- Don't exaggerate
  - You will get found out
- Include some education (beyond HS)
  - Use certifications or classes you've taken if you don't have something else
  - If you have nothing - take an online class and add that
- Drop Names
  - Companies
  - Individuals
- This is what would be included in your introduction if you were giving a commencement speech - people want to know that others trust you... so they can trust you

<u>The point is</u>: when you're done reading a bio... people feel like you have something to say & they should listen. You can include your current and past positions, but only as much as is beneficial to describe the persona that is an "expert in his/her field"

The point of a biography is that some people are only willing to do business with someone that is like them - fill it out as completely as possible, because you never know what fact you may have in common with your next best connection. You can include pieces of your current position, but only as much as is beneficial to describe the persona that is an "expert in his/her field"

Game: Memorize Anything

After writing out "Your Story" it's a good idea to learn it in such a way that you can access how to tell it "on the fly", when it is time to tell "Your Story"

a. **Create a series of images for each of the main points.**
b. **Develop bizarre mental transitions or morphing from one image to the next.** *(the crazier the better; because if you see a metallic purple monster truck with flames pass you—it will be harder to forget than a blue car)*
c. **Tell your story with the images and the transitions forward.**
d. **View the same movie (images and transitions) backward.**
e. **Repeat the movie forward and backward 2x, and you have it.**

*Tell it the same way every time so you know what people have heard and pick up from the middle. Just because it's your story doesn't mean that you will remember the main points every time without **using your script**.*

Draw out Your Story **Mental Memorization Movie**:

Know How Computers Translate your Brand

The internet is unforgiving. If you create the right (or wrong) attention—there is always the potential that it will never go away. We all see ourselves as our own celebrity. DON'T BE A CLICHÉ. We have created a society that praises self-induced narcissism (when we think everything is about us), and cultivate it as a form of self-confidence. Selfishness as confidence is a lie.

Your target doesn't browse the internet and engage social media to be slipped an advertisement.

...they go on the web *for what is important to them at that time*; respect that.

Create the right type of attention:

- **Use gathering tools.** There are services that will alert you when a specific phrase or word is used on a new blog post or website. There are also hashtag (#word) or keyword searches on social media networks and websites. If you search words that are specific to your target client, you can strike up a dialog as content is posted (that is complementary to your expertise), and is interesting enough (to your target) for them to write it.

- **Choose your resources.** When you locate someone who shares a common target audience, it's wise to engage their content, because your comments on their platform are visible to those you are trying to reach. Does their brand reflect the brand you are creating? If their expertise and their referrals are something that you would like to have access to; introduce yourself and offer to write a guest blog post on their site. As you engage other's content, you're getting your expertise in front of your target audience without having to give the time that is required to create or maintain that website. **Keep in mind that as you connect yourself with other's brands, your brand is being defined by your associations.**

- **Distribute content.** Use websites, landing pages, blogs, social media, email, text blast, video channels, podcasts, TV shows you watch, forums, groups, everything... Turn whatever you are doing into attractive content. Whether you use multiple social networks or only use one—look for excuses to offer expertise. Not all content needs to be business (and shouldn't be, because that's boring). Give a review of a show you just watched, share a picture of a great outfit, or engage friends while you're watching a game. Create and distribute content - and be fun about it.

It's a pretty simple process: 1. Share information, 2. Select wisely the brands to which you attach yourself - and attach, 3. Distribute enjoyable content. One, two, three, and attract the right type of attention.

The "simple process" of turning created and engaged content into a lead requires more of an intentional system than making comments or sharing a picture. *Attracting the right kind of attention requires a macro-level understanding of the mechanics and process of sales (later in this guide).*

Be Polite!

In my lifetime the concept of political correctness has ran headlong into countless generations of permissible (and recommended) language. There are jokes that were funny, until our culture was able to point out they were at the expense of a group of people. There are jokes that are celebrated today that will be seen as horribly offensive... tomorrow. Women were little more than the property of their husband 100 years ago, and today jokes that talk about how a husband needs mothering more than the children are common. Regardless of political correctness - politeness doesn't go out of style. Don't make a joke today that will read like the antics of the civil rights movement-ish... in another decade or two.

10 Rules to not posting something stupid

One, **be yourself.**

Mirroring is one of the greatest skills a salesperson has (addressed in later section), but it should never be used at the expense of being yourself. The moment we give an effort to be like someone else, we have wasted everyone's time and killed any reason others should give us attention.

If you like one musician and despise another, don't pretend that you like what you don't - simply to connect with someone who does; because that's unsustainable. Be willing to engage in conversation about that music; be polite about it. You also don't have to push your preferences on others (because they usually don't care). They don't know you, and if you're just being yourself - they can respect that.

Two, **you are what you type.**

If you are in a bad mood and you type something a little sassy or ugly—it will represent you as much once you're in a good mood as it does when you typed it. If you type things that are pleasant, kind, and decent; you are pleasant, kind, and decent.

Also, be aware that a business correspondence is read by many more eyes than whomever you send it to. Many times emails are forwarded or printed and copied for the final decision maker to review. Just because the person you work with on the proposal is silly, sassy or borderline inappropriate doesn't mean you won't look unreliable when your words are printed out.

Three, **make others feel important (sincerely).**

This is a tricky line to walk, because false sincerity is ugly and worse than not trying. True sincerity is beautiful. It makes others feel important. Even a humble person likes to feel valued. When you make them feel important, you're backing up a part of them that we all want others to know - and believe.

Rule of Thumb: Send a Note

A traditional point of etiquette is: when you have something sincere to express, you send them a note. *You don't have to write a personal note (like you did 50 to 70 years ago) to each encounter, but a note after an event or a Happy Birthday to each of your clients on social media is a kind gesture that places your name in front of everyone they know.*

If you want to send a personal note, there are great automation websites and handwritten note services that are waiting to help you at a minimum cost of time and money. There's little that compares (as far as percentage of time the message is read) to a handwritten note.

Four, **be careful and intentional using ALL CAPITAL LETTERS.**

This is text's version of yelling. Rarely is there a place in business for yelling; sometimes, but rarely. Actually, there are plenty of reasons to yell in business, but few long term benefits will come from it. All capitals do give a wonderful tool to give emphasis to one word in a sentence, but it's usually best to use *italic* rather than ALL CAPITALS.

Sales Tip: Intonation

Much of this book is dedicated to tracking and using non-verbal communication. Typically, the words given emphasis are the best way to understand the emotional state of the speaker. Be sure you use intonation on purpose.

- She took the purse
- **SHE** took the purse
- She **TOOK** the purse
- She took **THE** purse
- She took the **PURSE**

It's easy to lose focus during communication. As soon as you catch yourself not enjoying the time during a sale, pay attention to your intonation to guard how you say what you say… and smile. *(relax)*

Five, **avoid racy humor and profanity.**

The problem is, racy humor and profanity changes with time. My mom was raised in a part of St. Louis that was not culturally diverse. My family had specific words that they would use for different ethnicities. Some of which were derogatory and some were not intended to be negative, that's just the word used to describe that ethnicity. Culture has changed. If you use some words today… you'd probably lose your job and the respect you aim to attain.

We have not yet reached the equilibrium of a healthy social balance. Today, there's nothing wrong with certain ethnicities making incredibly racist jokes that degrade their own or certain other ethnicities—as long as he or she is a certain ethnicity. This will most likely change in the next decades. Web content doesn't go away. If you choose to engage in humor that is "funny" today, realize it may be destructive tomorrow.

Page 44 of 250

Six, **wait to reply until you're no longer angry.**

If you're angry; stop and pause. Close your computer, do something else and come back to it later. An ugly statement in the moment can do harm with unending ripple effects.

Seven, **give unsolicited endorsements.**

Everybody likes to be endorsed. Everybody likes to get a referral. Best way to get a referral from your network is to give them one. When you visit a local business, give them a positive review. You can even let them know that you did it and give them permission to share it.

Eight, **never criticize, condemn, or complain.**

Nobody cares, nobody cares, nobody cares. Often the best advice you can get is: **shut up and go on with your day.** The last thing you want is to connect with a new client whose best friend owns the business that you gave a horrible review to (it's tied to your personal brand).

Nine, **be genuinely interested in other people.**

Talk in terms of other's interests. If you learn to pay attention to others, they become more and more interesting. The more I've learned about how the brain functions (and how people interact with each other), the more entertaining people have become to me.

People are interesting. Sometimes you have to wade through a bit of the mire to get to the points of interest, but as my grandma used to say, "Chew up the meat and spit out the bones." **Enjoy people's peculiar brand of crazy and eventually they may come to appreciate yours.**

Ten, **Listen.**

The willingness and ability to listen more than you talk is like a power that you can develop and hold over those around you. If you are willing to be the one that listens (without slipping into a conversational slumber of disinterest) ... the more you really understand what is being communicated - the more **this will function like a superpower**. Read what others are saying. Engage the words they're speaking, as well as what they meant to say. If you let people talk long enough, they'll tell you how they want you to sell them. **Listen to what's being said and guide them where you want them to go.**

Sales Tip: The benefit is in the hearing, not the speaking

It sounds like an impossible thing to do, but the ability to listen (verbally and non-verbally) while you're speaking is a powerful 2.0 type communication tool. There have been countless times that I've been certain I spoke with accuracy and still the recipient was on a totally different page.

If you're listening with your eyes, you can see things like; look at where the other person's feet are pointing. It's likely that they are pointing their feet in the direction they want to go. Door? Phone? Computer? Contract?

Tracking where they look off in wonder (as you are speaking), what parts of the conversation receive an "OK", and other responses will allow you to know whether your audience is with you (or not). If you're the one confirming agreement on each step of the way throughout the sales process, you are allowed (and many times expected) to lead them to the close.

Make certain your audience is hearing what you're speaking.

code:tree

Define your target client

In our world (that holds inclusion of everyone as a virtue), selecting a target client is difficult, because (by its very nature) a specified focus is a *deselection of everyone else*. The reality is that you are selecting a focus for activity - not a parameter that must be attained before allowing inclusion. A target client doesn't mean you refuse to consider clients who are outside of your niche. **It does mean that you clearly describe the characteristics that separate your target from everyone else, and that you articulate why you are the best option for that client.** If you aim at everything you hit nothing. Often we lie to ourselves by defining our intended target - after we see what we hit. **A target client is merely a focused description; designating an optimum fit, but it is vital.**

Sales Tip: Which clients to focus on?

<u>Previous or current paying clients</u> who were <u>enjoyable to work with</u> yet required the <u>least time</u> and pay the <u>most money</u> create a profitable and sustainable model. There are often auxiliary target clients who are not the focus, but should be recognized when encountered. If there are certain products or services that have a quick close timeline (or possibility of automating the entire sales cycle): ask the closing question upfront (when someone is interested in that product or service). Direct them to where they can solve the problem without you—and move on. Many times this type of 'sale' is a wonderful self-funded lead generation channel.

It is deliciously tempting to describe target clients that you wish to attract and sign up as clients, even though up till now... you have no clients like this target. **STOP IT**. **Design your target client around past successes that have paid you money**, not wishes. To choose where you're heading you must accept where you've been. Start with remembering your favorite and least favorite clients. Ask yourself:

- Which clients hold your best and worst memories? Why?
- What details do you remember about them?
- How much did you make on this client?
- Did they give any referrals or were they a standalone client?
- If every client had to be modeled after just one deal, which one would it be?

Global Issue Online and Local Target Markets

The digital age has not yet reached an equilibrium in which local and online businesses play nicely together. Many online stores function more like a pick pocket - than fair competition (and vice versa). E-commerce requires no physical contact for someone to buy, which removes overhead cost. Face to face businesses can use the information on a website without ever giving them business. Compound that with the fact that many online stores are run by suppliers (wholesaler to the face to face business); the customer can often get a price that would be unsustainable for their local shop. Shoppers still seek personal face to face advice (we like to see and touch a product before buying), but we want to pay wholesale prices. *The electronic age will be owned by those who can harness the in-person and electronic realms seamlessly.*

Who they are (Quick Brainstorming Session)

1. What are the steps to describing your Target Client?

First thing you need to come to grips with is that if you are going to have a target client, that requires your **de-selection** of everyone else to be your target client

This is not an all or nothing, this is merely a **focus** for whom you are aiming at.

Categorize your favorite (& least favorite) clients:

Client Name:

_____

Good or Bad:_____

Why do you remember them?

_____

How much did you make on this client directly: _____

by referral? _____

Client Name:

_____

      Good or Bad:_____

Why do you remember them?

_____

How much did you make on this client directly: _____

      by referral? _____

Client Name:

_____

      Good or Bad:_____

Why do you remember them?

_____

How much did you make on this client directly: _____

      by referral? _____

List the clients that you've made the **most money** on:

Name of Client: Approximate Profit:

1. _____ _____
2. _____ _____
3. _____ _____
4. _____ _____
5. _____ _____

List the clients (or types of client/product or service) that you've make the **least money**:

Name of Client: Approximate Profit:

1. _____ _____
2. _____ _____
3. _____ _____
4. _____ _____
5. _____ _____

List the prospects that you spent the **most amount of time** on, but **didn't** make the sale:

Name of Client: Approximate Time:

1. _____ _____
2. _____ _____
3. _____ _____
4. _____ _____

List the prospects that you spent the **least amount of time** on, but **made** the sale:

Name of Client: Approximate Time:

1. _____ _____
2. _____ _____
3. _____ _____

What are the common characteristics of the clients that made the **greatest profit**?

Name of Client: Approximate Profit:

1. _____   _____
2. _____   _____
3. _____   _____
4. _____   _____
5. _____   _____

What are the common characteristics of the **dead prospects** that **took the most** time?

Name of Client: Approximate Time:

1. _____   _____
2. _____   _____
3. _____   _____
4. _____   _____
5. _____   _____

What are the common characteristics of the **closed clients** that **took the least** time?

Name of Client: Approximate Time:

1. _____   _____
2. _____   _____
3. _____   _____
4. _____   _____
5. _____   _____

What **products or services** you've sold that had the **least** time & greatest profit?

	Name of Client:	Approximate Profit:
1.	_____	_____
2.	_____	_____
3.	_____	_____
4.	_____	_____
5.	_____	_____

Finish these statements:

- At this point if I could choose my Target Client they...

_____

_____

- The Product/Service that has the highest profit to time invested ratio is/are:

_____

_____

_____

After Brainstorming Sessions...

1. Filter the Categories that your Target Client can be grouped into:

Once you've had a chance to review your most memorable clients, begin to construct the widest 'top of the funnel' client type categories. Beginning of the sales pipeline/funnel:

- What category of client did you make the most money on?

- What prospect types demanded a lot of time, but never paid a dime?

- Which leads turned into quick and easy sales that required almost no time or energy, and yet created income?

- Which clients brought the greatest profit, and yet didn't allow you time to do anything else while they were making a decision?

It is obvious that if a business is based on clients that take **minimal time but produce maximum income**—it will succeed (at least financially). Financial success may be the standard used on Wall Street, but long term profitability requires calculation of more details than just the dollars collected. Burnout and training replacements carry a high price tag (especially when the burnout being replaced is you).

2. Assess your Target Client's motivations:

Through exercises like those listed above; the primary income channels should begin to rise to the top, and those who specialize in being headaches should be allowed to sink to the bottom. As you work your way down the selection funnel, there are a couple primary points of consideration:

- **What was the real need the client had filled by giving you business?** Don't over simplify this point by listing what was on your sales order. One person may purchase to alleviate pain, while others may buy the exact same product to confirm they have the authority to make a wise decision (even though they may not fully understand the wisdom behind the decision). Comprehend the motivation that justified their feeling good about giving you money. Look for consistencies among the target categories that you are designing as your target.

- **What current product best fits with these client's motivation?** The reason people purchase a piece of equipment may change over time. A system that was wildly successful when you were a sales person may not work at all - now that you are a sales manager. Your frustration is that you think your team is being lazy, when they are working harder than you in an effort to make you happy... all the while doing what needs to be done to get paid. *What do you offer today that will most securely fit the fulfillment of the need resolved?*

3. Describe and Define Your Target Client:

This is not merely a generalized overview of feeling or impression you have when you're around that optimum client. This is a specific description of a fictional (but visualized) person who is described in such detail that they can be sought out and recognized when introduced. Once defined, this person is foundational in the design and creation of your communication style, and this person is used as the basis for the system you will follow walking a lead from their expression of interest to a point of decision. Though there are literally hundreds of categories that can be used in defining your target client, create a well-rounded description that makes sense to you and others.

- **Personal demographic** such as relationship status, gender, age, family make up, etc.
- **Business demographic life** including size of business, employees, industry, annual revenue, etc.

- **My target client's personal lifestyle** which includes favorite foods, clothing style, vacations destinations, hobbies and free-time activities, etc. *(Facebook?)*

4. Assess your Reality:

Even if you only consider client groupings that you have experienced past success, there is still a chance that the target niche you are aiming at may not be realistic. There is a level of sustainability that is required. If your reality isn't honestly assessed, your target client will need to be re-defined every few months... which will consistently take you away from the end goal of running your business. Be completely honest with yourself:

- **Are there enough people in my target niche that need what I have to offer?**

- **Which competitors aim at the same niche?**

  - **Can you share the market share, or how will you take over their share?**

  - **Is there a specific segment of that niche you will specialize in more than your competition?**

- **Can they afford what I'm selling?**

  - **Is your price point too high for them to afford?**

  - **Is your price point too low for them to assume quality?**

- **Do I have access to my Target Clients?**

It's OK to have more than one target niche, but not to have multiple focal points for any single marketing campaign. Select one target client and design all your branded campaign specific marketing collateral around that one target. There is a good chance that the target client you select will have multiple subsets. Create a target client and move forward with a specific focus.

Reading Patterns & Habits

Every person in this world is wonderfully complex. At times; the complexities can drive us crazy, because we assume current experience is going to reflect historic encounters.

The trick is to recognize which assumptions/frames (through which we view what is happening) are based on real experiences... which can't be completed in the time that we have available... and which are able to be addressed productively... and most importantly - they're able to be taken down or altered. OK, maybe that one was a run on sentence.

Four types of Patters & Habits to read:

One: Physical Tells.

Two: Generalization.

Three: Deletion versus Categorization.

Four: Distortion.

Be sensitive to your surroundings.

"The most important thing in communication is to hear what's not being said," - quote I've heard attributed to Peter Drucker.

Observation and Interpretation fit together.

- **Observation** is what comes in with your five senses, and
- **Interpretation** is what you do with it through the system of communication, behavior, and the creation of new filters.

Developing your people reading skills:

1. Start with paying attention to posture.

What is their default position? What is yours? What do they do as they get out of their default position? Why? You have to figure out what their default position is; because you need a baseline from which to gauge how they deviate... if you track the baseline and deviations.

Examples:

"They" might be someone who's really laid back, and so the concept of tilting their head is an extreme expression of interest.

"They" may be ADHD, and the fact that they stand up in the middle of the meeting means nothing other than the fact that their ADHD got the best of them.

> ### You have to have a <u>baseline</u>.

> ### Pay attention to their <u>resting position</u>, and changes.

2. Track their physical tells

Once you have a standard of baseline physical actions, you can track their unconscious movements to understand when, to what extent, and how drastically they are altering their baseline posture which typically indicates their own internal anchors going off.

What is it that they are communicating by these subtle variations of their body? ...their breath and voice?

What you look for:

- Location and Depth of their Breathing
- Gestures & Jiggles & Twitches

- Taps of Appendages
- Pitch, Tempo, Rhythm & Volume of their Voice
- Eye Movements (this is a cool tool)
- Foot Position, etc.

In every behavior, there's a positive intention.

Everyone does what they do **_on purpose_**. Even if it negatively affects the rest of their life, the anchor (that is dragging to alter their actions) was created and has grown out of some positive intention. Every evil is a perversion of good. People make the best choices available to them... at the time... so they think and believe... or they wouldn't have created the anchor.

- At that moment...

 - with their history...

 - knowing what they know...

 - in their belief structure when it's created...

 - with the resources at their disposal...

 - viewed from their frame of reference...

People make the best choices available to them.

Give your energy and effort to uncovering the positive motivation that is the springboard for others' behavior, and respond to that. It's the shortest route out of whatever is broken.

Sales Tip: Overcoming Objections

There are a couple reasons that a prospect will withhold information; **either they are fearful** or **they are still not convinced**, or **both**. If you ask the right questions you will be able to filter these two options.

1. *If they are scared, pushing may in fact lose you a sale that won't and can't happen until tomorrow—no matter how great of sales skills*

you have today. Your pushing only showed the client that they would enjoy working with someone else.

2. *If they are not convinced, you may have missed a legitimate piece of your sales pitch.*

A quick reference of what points they have agreed on up to this point is useful when deletions appear to be unfounded. Get back to the last checkpoint or baseline, and rebuild the foundation from there.

These tools all fit together.

The resources that we manage are more expansive than our world has ever known (at least since we started keeping written record allowing one generation to build on the knowledge of one or more previous generations). ***TOOL: you can review personal pictures from family vacations, personal journals (blogs) and company news in a three-minute appointment prep research session.***

- *Questions are used to fill in the gaps and clarify your understanding of the current and historic status of whomever you're meeting). Even though it is necessary to generalize when going through the Pre-Appointment Research... every person and situation has its own set of factors that make it distinct.*

- *That is one example of a situation that you need to use Generalization, but (when used in the proper settings) generalization can add clarity, simplicity, and focus to our lives.*

- *With tools like Generalization, if we recognize and use a set list of existing tools we (and others) use, we're able to guess what their next move, response, concern, etc - might be.*

Define: Generalization

Whatever we encounter—whether positive or negative—we pull the necessary pieces out as quickly as possible, strip away the (seemingly unimportant) peripheral details, and generalize it. It's placed into a category of our thinking that is based on past encounters, variables and people... experiences. This tool of reason is Generalization.

This is necessary

Once we piece the details together - we have understanding.

Three types of Generalization:

1) Necessity and Possibility: There is a statement of need referencing a point that is fully outside of anyone's control that is directly affecting the decision.

- A sample is, *"This can't happen."*

- Why Address this: Absolute generalizations of this fashion are only beneficial to address if the entire deal needs to be placed on the table with a poker type "all in" play… and it becomes a win or go home moment.

- Possible clarifying statement, "Describe for me what will take place if this goes through"

- What you don't do: Don't believe the statement is a Fact. I don't have to tell someone that they are lying, if we both know they are lying. If someone believes that these types of Necessity and Possibility generalization are facts - they're in a prison of this thought… because the words of a generalization are designed to be exaggerated for effect and aren't supposed to be fact… unless you have no creativity in problem solving. **There *are* times** using this type of generalization… is the only smart move. In business, it's better to lose early - if you're going to lose anyway. You're being a good manager of your resource of time. Save the time it will take to get a "No", and get on to your next client.

Rule of Thumb: Negative Absolutes

- People who commonly give negative absolutes like "can't" and "never" may appear to enjoy verbal banter in this line of talk (with unchangeable and negative absolutes), but it's typically self-destructive.

- There's actually a great poem "Can't" by Edgar Albert Guest that's worth reading.

2) Universal Statements: A perspective is expressed that is too vast to be possible, but has a root that is directly affecting the decision.

- A sample is, *"I'll try to reach them, but he's never here."*

- Why Address this: if you think they are in control of whether you overcome this communicated hurdle. If their generalization is going to continue hindering your progress and ability to make contact with the necessary parties to close the deal.

- Possible clarifying statement, "Does he work from home?"

- What you don't do: Don't respond with a generalization that is equally ludicrous (in frustration). Everyone involved in the conversation knows that the person you are talking to is simply exaggerating; due to their lack of control of something. If you ask a clarifying question—make sure it is sensible, clear, direct, and watch their response as you're saying it - in case there's something else provoking this generalization.

3) Pre-guessing: This is co-dependent pre-judging.

- A sample is, *"If they cared for this company, they'd be here."*

- Why Address this: If the pre-judging is evidently a hindrance to finishing up the deal. Also, if there's a sense that the contact won't make a decision without others joining later.

- Possible clarifying statement, "I'm willing to wait if they could be corralled to meet with us today."

- What you don't do: Don't lose perspective. Don't' forget why you're there. Also, don't forget your place in the room. If it's a point that people are indifferent to the decision (like what's inferred in this example)—don't hold off the deal until others are available (unless they are the signer). If you think your contact won't move—don't get caught up in your contact's annoyance and internal bickering. Ugly actions are sticky, and usually don't make us better for touching them.

Four types of deletion:

It is seductive to think I'm above these types of generalization; even though (as you read these words), you are deleting (generalizing) all that is not in whatever categories you are using to file (or dispose of) this information. We are always filing certain communications and deleting other (assumedly unneeded) points. That is why it is beneficial to routinely go through these tools/training (even though it's the same content), because items you tuned out (deleted) last time may be life changing six months later.

Define: Deletion vs categorization

We are constantly focusing on some parts and tuning out others... *always*. Our selection of what to delete and what to categorize is based on previously set factors and categories. Clarity can be found when the unrelated points of connection are exposed and cut (but it can be painful as well).

1) Simple deletion: They have deleted a piece of their statement, and you only hear half of a thought.

- A sample is, *"I'm worried."*

- Why Address this: Some information is missing and without this, or these details there's no way to move forward. If it's not vital (like most generalizations), drop it.

- Possible clarifying question, "Are you worried about something with this deal or is it something else?"

- What you don't do: Don't guess what they're worried about and stop there. Either dismiss their worry as not having to do with the business at hand, or address it with a specific piece of information or insight you are seeking in the form of a leading question.

2) **Comparative deletion**: They have deleted the source of their concern and offered a metaphor as a source of reference rather than the actual point of concern.

- A sample is, *"It's not a good idea to rock the boat."*
- Why Address this: If the only way to accomplish the desired end goal is to take the time to go through some discussions that the client has carefully avoided. RARE!
- Possible clarifying question, "Did something happen when people felt like you rocked the boat? How is this situation like that one?"
- What you don't do: Start to answer why 'rocking the boat' is necessary, or why it's not a problem. There is a better than average chance that you do not have all the details that went into the expression of concern about this un-leveled boat.

3) **Point of reference deletion**: They have deleted an involved party or entity.

- A sample is, *"I'll get in so much trouble..."*
- Why Address this: When there is something missing that is a needed point of reference (a person or an organization) of whom you may be ignorant. It may be valid to see how they're involved in the decision process or effected/affected by the decision. You may not be talking to the final decision maker (whether you think you are or not).
- Possible clarifying question, "Is there a source to that worry, or is it someone specific?"
- What you don't do: Don't assume they're not the one making the final decision, or the one with the authority. This is a

commonly used tool. It's also possible that they are the gatekeeper who is put in place to waste your time, but many times a conscientious leader will express concern for how his or her organization will respond to change. It's not always negative. A wrong and insulting assumption will kill your rapport—and probably your deal.

4) Floating verb deletions: There is a verb that was used, but no noun is offered for the action to be tied to.

- A sample is, *"I always mess this up."*

- Why Address this: If it's possible that the missing noun could be a factor in the final decision. Also, if there's been an ongoing hesitation that may be hovering around this noun.

- Possible clarifying question, "What about this decision doesn't feel settled?" Ask them to fill in the blanks.

- What you don't do: When someone is willing to make a statement with that type of transparency and uncomfortable personal self-disclosure (in a negative sense), don't try to be a psychologist and address the root issue. There's really no place for this level of personal self-disclosure in a business meeting, because we don't have the relational worth (or often we also don't have the time) necessary to unravel whatever is in a knot. This is a good time to make sure you want them as a client.

Five types of distortion:

Accept that you are always distorting what you take in and be willing to back track. We all only have one visualized memory to translate our experience through. We all function through bias. Simplifying or synopsizing an experience is a form of distorting... to get to the essence of what was being communicated. These are good tools.

Define: Distortion

Distorting facts is usually intended to create clarity through metaphor or re-phrasing.

Distortion replaces the details on the assumption that (from the perspective of the speaker) a different set of details (spoken or unspoken) will be common enough to create clarity and understanding.

Don't get caught drifting into the presumption that any distortion (no matter how applicable) won't break down in confusion—eventually.

1) Cause and effect: An unreal effect is attributed to a point or person that could not be held responsible for the effect.

- A sample is, *"She makes me crazy."*

- Why Address this: If there is a way to use this to your benefit and create a sense of "I'm on your side."

- Possible clarifying question, "What does she do?" (*careful here*)

- What you don't do: Don't dismiss the statement, because you are dismissing him/her. There are real emotions being communicated, and there is no possible benefit from pushing back against the statement.

2) Mind Reading: This includes statements assuming knowledge of internal truths that are held by a 3rd party. That they are able to read a person's mind.

- A sample is, *"He thinks he's always right."*

- Why Address this: If either of the parties involved in the mind reading are vital to the final decision making. If it's addressed it needs to be in a completely nebulous manner. No one enjoys being caught in a lie.

- Possible clarifying question, "How's that?"
- What you don't do: Anytime you engage in a discussion that is based on a 'mind reading' statement, you are cooperating in a fictional (and delusional) process. If you use this as an opportunity to gain insight into someone you are in negotiation with; do it quickly and get out.

3) Faulty Relationship: This is when there is a false and usually exaggerated connection between parties.

- A sample is, *"I screwed up this appointment—I suck at this."*
- Why Address this: This one is common in daily business, because we use self-talk. If you do have someone who is making a false connection (*and* effects your deal)—that may be a time to address it.
- Possible clarifying question, "I don't see that. What am I missing?"
- What you don't do: Don't commiserate - even if you have perfect reason to do so. It's seductive to jump into it, because having someone to partner with in the expression of the frustrations of daily life is addicting. We all have rough days. Unless the commiseration is based on creating rapport and furthering the deal—you are engaging in activity that is counterproductive to what you're there to do. Stay on task.

4) Opinions as Fact: This is probably the most common distortion we experience. There are opinions we hold so dear that we assume we are completely accurate if we present them as facts (based on our beliefs). Societies function though these types of generalizations.

- A sample is, *"Web marketing is a waste of time and money."*
- Why Address this: If the opinion is detrimental to your cause—you should address it. If it's not detrimental or if it is

not connected to your end purpose, you should leave it alone no matter how dearly you hold your opinion. Remember, it takes time to change another's thoughts - it never just happens because they had not considered the wonderful insight you may offer them :-).

- Possible clarifying question, "Have you wasted time on this before?" or possibly, "What does your staff currently do that wastes their time while they're on the clock that's not productive for your company?", but provocation (as a tool) usually produces more pain than benefit (in the long run).

- What you don't do: Don't point out that the fact that they are stating is actually opinion. There's no benefit to pointing out the obvious and defending an opinion only solidifies the conviction. This was important enough to keep it short.

5) Verb as a Noun: This is when someone uses... a verb as a noun.

- A sample is, *"There's too much confusion here."*

- Why Address this: The greatest benefit for recognizing and addressing this distortion is that the noun being omitted is usually the speaker or an influencing factor. There is a missing "we" or "I" with "am confused" that is being admitted, but is blocked by pride. Rather than owning it, they blame an impersonal verb. That poor verb - it's been taken advantage of since middle school.

- Possible clarifying question, "What are the main points of confusion... is there one?" Regardless of the words used here, these are open doors to uncovering final decision points. Look for an opening to facilitate the deal.

- What you don't do: Don't give focus to the point of brokenness ("confusion" in the example).

Sales Tip: Use Reset Questions

A couple of provoking questions that have helped my sales process:

1) Magic Wand: If you're having troubles figuring out what the prospect actually wants by getting to the heart of the issue—propose, "If you had a magic wand you could waive over the current issues and circumstance—what would you have in place?"

2) Compare and Contrast. What are the alternatives to what we're discussing? If you choose not to move forward in this situation, what is going to happen? **Describe it to me.** Push for clarity and detail, but as with any time you push - be their pressure release valve if you see the pressure being too great. I find pointing out my faults (picking on myself) puts others at ease.

Allow them to explain to you why this is a deal that they need you to close to make their life better. Listen and Direct the right Questions.

Many times people don't make a decision... because the decision making process is more painful than the issue being resolved. So have them describe it. Listen.

The point for these exercises is; let the people that are responsible for the final decision start to describe what they're looking for. Engage them and provoke as much detail as possible.

Mastery Level People Reading

There are no answers here - only hints. There are some people who are inverse on every point addressed here (and function that way for any number of reasons). Others may only be inverse on one clue or another. These are clues that can be tracked; giving a foundation of reading the person across from you, and informing an educated guess when the time calls for it.

When you are in face to face position, people typically respond with their eyes long before they say anything, so that's a good place to start. When we activate a non-essential motor function, it is usually in response to whatever we are thinking at the time. This can be powerful.

SIDE TO SIDE CLUES TO WHETHER MEMORIES OR CREATIVITY IS BEING USED:

- o The right side of our brain is the creative side
    - If <u>THEY LOOK</u> to *YOUR LEFT* they are looking to their right, which will activate the right side of their brain (which is <u>creative</u>).
- o The left side is the facts and figures side.
    - If <u>THEY LOOK</u> to *YOUR RIGHT* they are looking to their left, which will activate the left side of their brain (which is facts and figures). Facts are typically <u>memories</u>.

UP & DOWN CLUES TO WHICH SENSORY CHANNEL IS PREFERRED:

- o Eyes are at the top of the body
    - A recalled Visual; looks up and/or touch your eyes or play with glasses

- Ears are to the side of the head
  - A recalled Audio is when you look to the side
- Hands and legs are below the neck
  - Feeling is when you look down (toward your hands).
- Considering Taste and Smell are uncommon to highlight in business conversation, using Touch words when Taste or Smell clues are shown (like touching the mouth) is common.

These seem almost silly, but we are physical creatures and have default reactions that are sensory based. This is not an absolute science, but a great tool to develop and use to stay a step ahead. *note; sometimes people have the sides switched... you can see it based on what they're talking about (art not a science).*

Campaign Mechanisms

Farming: activity that pays off like planting seed in the fall to eat food next summer

1. **Keywords: the starting point**

2. **On-page/Off-page Optimization**

3. **Analyze and Adjust**

Fishing: activity that catches a big one, but takes time to understand the target

1. **Select Location** (Choose which Hole to fish today)

2. **Create and Distribute Content** (Choose the Bait to use)

3. **Turn Traffic into Real People** (The Cast)

4. **Socially Engage People** (Set the Hook)

5. **Analyze and Adjust moment by moment** (In the Net)

Hunting: identify target, plan attack, pursue, eat (when fishing becomes 1 on 1)

1. What are you currently doing?

2. Identify Your Target Action

3. Campaign Design

4. Schedule Activity

5. Negotiation Preparation

6. Analyze and Adjust (weekly-monthly)

****
****

!!!SPECIAL NOTE!!!

Pay attention to the search engines guidelines because if you break them, you can get blacklisted to the point that you don't show up anywhere. It is worse than having a bad site. You are cut off and your domain doesn't show up *__anywhere__*. Play by the rules.

****
****

10 Step Campaign Builder Guide

Campaign Objective/outcome/objective/goal - defined:

- Collins English Dictionary: something that follows action; a result or consequence
  - **A goal** is always:
    - Something we want
      - *it's not necessarily something we desire*
    - "SMART" guidelines for goals says:
      - **S**: Specific
      - **M**: Measurable
      - **A**: Achievable
      - **R**: Realistic
      - **T**: Time-bound

  - While an **outcome** is: what we get as an **end result** for our actions

Your Campaign Objective is a specific end result or outcome,

<u>10 steps to ensure End Results or Outcome:</u>
1. State the End Result in POSITIVE terms
2. Make sure the End Result is COMPLETELY within your control
3. Write it down as SPECIFIC as possible
4. List (using all 5 senses) the EVIDENCE for completion
5. Consider the CONTEXT
6. Assess the RESOURCES required
7. Consider the BY-PRODUCTS of changed actions
8. Check the outcome's RIPPLE EFFECTS on the rest of your world
9. Write out CLARIFYING QUESTIONS for the 1st Step
10. Write down the NEXT outcome you will be allowed to do once this is complete

Currently Used

Brainstorm 60 seconds what you are currently doing for sales & marketing

Sales & Marketing Campaign/Task   **Why do you do this?**

_____   _____

_____   _____

_____   _____

_____   _____

_____   _____

_____   _____

_____   _____

_____   _____

_____   _____

_____   _____

_____   _____

Now go back and mark them with the following:
1. What is the purpose for each step?
    a. How much/many of desired results have you actually experienced *in the last 3 months* (for each)
2. Filter Process... which ones:
    a. Take the most time
    b. Create the most income
    c. Do you dislike
    d. Haven't created results

Why do you do it? What is the purpose?
- Get Sales (money changes hands)
- Get Leads (what do you do with them)
- Nurture Leads into Sales (Some lead nurturing can also end in referrals for sales - just as good)
- Build Brand Awareness (Which of the first two are going to benefit from awareness of your brand)
- Something else:

Step 1

1. **State the End Result in POSITIVE terms**

Write Down the Campaign Objective you are going to achieve. What is the end result going to be?

- Don't get stuck thinking of marketing or sales as the end for what you are doing.
    - You need to see the end as the result you want to see achieved.
    - If you market for the sake of marketing - you are only adding a task to you list.
        - You may as well have "read" or "surf the web" as tasks.

The end result/campaign objective is what gives purpose and focus to your marketing and sales actions.

When we use negative language we end up focusing on what we don't want rather than what we want. This is the opposite effect of what is intended. Don't underestimate the power of this step. **You get what you focus on.**

Use the positive word list (following page) to complete the outcome.

_____

_____

_____

_____

_____

_____

Positive Alphabet of Options Words List

Acceptable, Beautiful, Complete, Determined, Excellent, Fair, Good, Heavenly, Intentionally, Justified, Keep, Long-term, Manage, Now, Open, Perfect, Quick, Right, Standard, Team, LOTS OF "U" WORDS ARE NEGATIVE... BUT IF YOU HAVE TO... Unbelievable, Victorious, Will, Xylophone (does any other word start with "X"?), Yes, Zenith.

Go and quit talking people out of liking you (we're drawn to the positive).

Step 2

1. State the End Result in POSITIVE terms
2. **Make sure the End Result is COMPLETELY within your control**

If it requires other people to do certain things, or not do certain things it's *not* an acceptable outcome.

Seven Steps to ensure your Sales from Marketing is completely within your control:

1. **Write out an intentional sales process or "Pipeline" (tool included)**

    a. Assess the existing pipeline you are using to get customers (write down each step/point of contact that takes place - from introduction/referral to 1st payment received)

    b. Highlight the steps that you can't get a client without

    c. Write the outline you follow on each step (with next step goal) and write the time that typically passes between each step

    d. Determine the pipeline length (time it takes to create a client from someone you meet today)

2. **Create your Quotas (tool included)**

    a. Enter ratios of activity to results for each piece of the quota

3. **Build, and Record scripts and tools for your Campaign/Pipeline (tool included)**

   a.   Include each step in the process

       i.   Those that you are meeting with the prospect
      ii.   Those that you are doing work with in prep or review
    iii.   Include points of decision with whether you want to continue or not.

4. **Categorize your prospect list by step in pipeline**

5. **Schedule a UNNEGOTIABLE pipeline follow up/reschedule process**

6. **Set up a calendar event to schedule "how you're doing" (monthly?)**

7. **Select three to five current clients that have signed up recently enough to remember the sales process "pipeline" they went through to become a client. (list them to use in this campaign design)**

       i.   Optimum client(s):

      _____

      ii.   Most distinct client(s):

      _____

    iii.   Target client(s):

      _____

Current Pipeline

Purpose of this exercise: If you meet a buyer today, how long is it going to take you to get paid?

Touch or Step in the Process	Your Next Step	Their Next Step	Days

- List every "touch" or step in the process of getting a prospect's information to getting paid.
  - Take the number of days listed in the right column and add them up. If you are in charge, this is how long you are asking them to wait to give you money.

QUESTIONS YOU AND YOUR SALES STAFF SHOULD ASK:
- What are the vital steps in this process?

- What do you absolutely NEED to know before making a decision to do business with them?
- What do you need to know about them to provide your service or product well?
- What can you cut out of your Pipeline, in order to streamline the decision process for the prospect?
- Why do you think moving the pipeline along is something that is only for your benefit?
  - Do you not believe you are good for the client?
  - Why not let them experience the benefit as soon as possible?
- Which of these steps do you have a Take Away?
- Which "touches" have a script written? How about Materials that are used each time?

Quota (replace the names below with the stages in your pipeline)

1. <u>Fill in the number in section one that will populate the answers you will need to calculate everything else.</u>

    a. How many *closing* appointments to get a sale?
        i. *Answer:* _____

    b. How many *qualifying* appointments to get a *closing* appointment?
        i. *Answer:* _____

    c. How many *introductions* to get a *qualifying* appointment?
        i. *Answer:* _____

    d. How many *leads* needed to get an *introduction* appointment?
        i. *Answer:* _____

    e. How much money (new business) do you need to bring in per month?
        i. *Answer:* _____

    f. How much do you make on your average sale?
        i. *Answer:* _____

    g. Number of sales reps for which you provide leads?
        i. *Answer:* _____

2. Run the pipeline equation: (write in the info from section 1 - based on lettered question)

- a: _____ x b: _____
  = **Qualifying appointments per mo.:** _____

- Qualifying appointments per mo.:_____ x c:_____
  = **Introductions per mo.:** _____

- Introductions per mo.: _____ x d:_____
  = Number of leads to get a sale: _____

- e: _____ / f: _____
  = Number of sales needed per month: _____

    ○ Number of leads to get a sale: _____

    x Number of sales needed per month:_____

    Leads needed per month: _____

QUOTAS: Break it down to weekly quotas:
To determine weekly quota from monthly number, divide by 4.33 because there are 13 weeks every three months. *If you would like to plan on taking every 13th week off - you should divide by 4 rather than 4.33*, but if you're not willing to actually take the 13th week off, don't pretend that you are going to give you an excuse to not hit your quota by having a higher quota than you actually have to hit. Quotas must be considered a nonnegotiable number you have to hit or you don't stop working. *Don't lie to yourself.*

- **Qualifying Appointments per mo. / 4.33 = Qualifying appointments per week:** _____
- **Introductory Appointments per mo. / 4.33 = Introductory Appointments per week:** _____
- **Leads per mo. / 4.33 = Leads per week:** _____
- **g:** _____ **x Leads per week:** _____ **= Number of leads you need to have each week:**
     Answer: _____

Pipeline Scripts Refinement [see: pg. 201 (to create a pipeline)]

The theory of using scripts is better than the experience. Most people are willing to look at the idea of automation and consider the time it would save; but when it comes down to it, they aren't willing to use the templates because creating a new process is too hard (in their imagination). Here's an exercise that will help you understand what the prospect hears and reads when they go through the sales process with you.

<u>After you have completed the pipeline flowchart (...pg. 201 has the guide)</u>

1. Set it in front of you
2. Set up a method to record what you say
   a. Use a laptop to record video - OR IF YOU DON'T' HAVE A VIDEO RECORDING DEVICE -
   b. Use a Phone or other audio recording device
   c. If you don't have one of those, call your voicemail for each of these steps to record what you say (without stopping during the practice pitch)
3. If possible (and you're brave) - get someone to be the customer in this role playing exercise
6. Start at the first item on the pipeline flowchart, and record your role play of that conversation
7. Make a transcription of the statement as you watch/listen to the recorded conversation
   a. Type out every word you said
      i. If you say "Uh" type "Uh", if you say "and well", type "and... well"

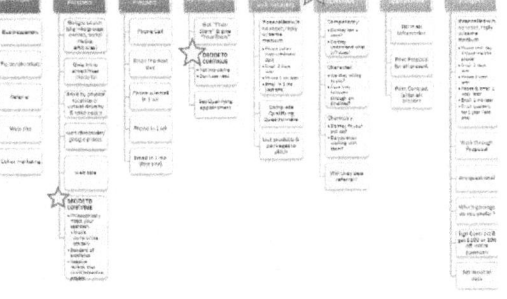

     b. This can be a painful exercise, but it is one of the only ways to filter the useless words from your pipeline conversations (pain), and what you record is what they will have to listen to
        i. If you force prospects to listen to you, it's worth the time to force yourself to listen

8. Take your transcription and edit it down to the thoughts/words that are necessary
     a. What communicates the point you are making
     b. What 'auto-pilot' statements do you use to fill the "thinking gaps"
     c. Do you do anything non-verbally or make noises that are distracting
     d. KNOW YOURSELF

9. Go on to the next conversation in the pipeline and record it as well. Repeat until you have recorded, transcribed, edited and fine-tuned every step in your pipeline. (Schedule this practice)

10. Once you have completed the entire pipeline, repeat it by recording your edited scripts & practice.
     a. This is an exercise that is beneficial at least annually
     b. Make a checklist and have someone keep you accountable for completing this action

No one likes this exercise, so if you don't have someone check up on you - it will never get done and you will continue bad habits (if you don't stay fine-tuned).

Step 3

1. State the End Result in POSITIVE terms
2. Make sure the End Result is COMPLETELY within your control
3. **Write it down as SPECIFIC as possible**

- **Outcomes that are too big:**
  - o When there are large end results you "just can't wrap your mind around", it may be necessary to break it down into a series of smaller jobs.
    - i. First look at the end result and create the steps that will be involved in achieving the outcome
    - ii. Answer "What stops me from having this outcome now" (or "what will stop me at that point") for each step

- **Outcomes that are too small**
  - o If they seem unimportant or not motivating enough, you may need to "chunk up" to a more important outcome that causes you to feel something
  - o If it's not clear why you are engaging in a certain activity, you may be confusing this step for step #4 (which is the sensory evidence of completion of the outcome) ... we'll get there soon

- **Write Down what your outcome again. What is the end result going to be?**
  - o Write it down with the basis (up to this point) of
    - Keep it positive
    - Make sure it's within your control
    - Keep it as specific as possible

New articulation of your outcome:

Step 4

1. State the End Result in POSITIVE terms
2. Make sure the End Result is COMPLETELY within your control
3. Write it down as SPECIFIC as possible
4. **List (using all 5 senses) the EVIDENCE for completion**

When you write down an outcome be certain to fill it up with sensory specific language. The more specific the feeling you have in describing the end result - the less likelihood of ending up with undesired results
- Visual (see)
- Audible (hear)
- Kinesthetic (feel)
    - I'm adding two others there, but they're definitely auxiliary
        - Gustatory (taste)
        - Olfactory (smell)

These lists include positive & negative for your future reference, but keep outcomes positive!

SEE	HEAR	FEEL	TASTE	SMELL
see	tell	feel	hungry	honey
look	sound	hard	honey	burnt
show	hear	cold	burnt	foul
clear	speak	balance	delicious	pine
view	silence	pain	garlicky	scent
read	listen	warm	sour	garlic
dark	volume	touch	nutty	dusty
appear	knock	soft	stale	onion
picture	bass	catch	vinegar	sour
eye	dialogue	motion	tasty	fumes
obvious	verbal	impression	alkaline	vapors
shape	quote	concrete	seasoned	floral
sight	announce	thrust	smoky	rotting
shadow	scream	excited	spicy	aroma
perspective	noisy	dull	acidic	fragrance
reveal	roar	relax	salty	sniff
glance	melody	tender	pungent	aromatic
dawn	articulate	grasp	gag	bouquet
focused	tenor	tense	fruity	smoky

What are the evidences of Campaign Objective completion?

When this end result is realized, I will **see or show**:

- _____
- _____
- _____
- _____
- _____
- _____
- _____

When this end result is realized, I will **hear or tell**:

- _____
- _____
- _____
- _____

When this end result is realized, I will **feel or touch**:

- _____
- _____

Step 5

1. State the End Result in POSITIVE terms
2. Make sure the End Result is COMPLETELY within your control
3. Write it down as SPECIFIC as possible
4. List (using all 5 senses) the EVIDENCE for completion
5. **Consider the CONTEXT**

This is essentially taking into consideration the framework of the end result when it comes to:

- Where:
  _____

- When:
  _____

- With Whom:
  _____

- Will this outcome effect only one part of life or be all encompassing?
  _____
  _____

- When do you want this outcome to be the only thing you are focusing on?
  _____
  _____

- Who do you want to see you in the light of this end result... only?
  _____
  _____
  _____

Context

Chart 1.

What are the stages to complete the outcome?	Approx. Date	Where it will take place	Permission needed

Chart 2.

Who will be involved in this process?	Who is vital to the outcome?	Effected by success of outcome?

Chart 3.

What circumstance do you not want this outcome to be present?

Step 6

1. State the End Result in POSITIVE terms
2. Make sure the End Result is COMPLETELY within your control
3. Write it down as SPECIFIC as possible
4. List (using all 5 senses) the EVIDENCE for completion
5. Consider the CONTEXT
6. **Assess the RESOURCES required**

PURPOSE: assess realistically whether the resources needed to achieve the outcome are worth the result
Resources needed during the process of this outcome:

- ## Internal:
  - o Skills:
  _____
  - o Knowledge:
  _____
  - o Understanding:
  _____
  - o Courage:
  _____
  - o Other:
  _____

- ## External:
  - o Money:
  _____
  - o Contacts:
  _____
  - o Equipment:
  _____
  - o Other:
  _____

Step 7

1. State the End Result in POSITIVE terms
2. Make sure the End Result is COMPLETELY within your control
3. Write it down as SPECIFIC as possible
4. List (using all 5 senses) the EVIDENCE for completion
5. Consider the CONTEXT
6. Assess the RESOURCES required
7. **Consider the BY-PRODUCTS of changed actions**

It is important to ensure that the outcome will preserve existing benefits of current actions or inactivity. There is a reason that things function in the manner that they do. There are perceived positive (real or not) results that come from the current status quo that will sabotage the outcome if they are not pacified.

List the possible by-product of current campaign actions, what might be lost and how it will be compensated.
EXAMPLE:

Existing Benefit:	I started a business to be in charge of my schedule
Sabotaging by-product:	If I don't hit my quota for the week, I won't stay late on a Friday - because no one will make me and I don't want to.
Resolution:	I will track my weekly introductions & qualifying appointment quota from Wednesday to Tuesday each week.
Resolution double check:	Am I willing to stay late on Tuesdays to hit my quota?
Context double check:	I've confirmed my office will be open late on Tuesdays & my spouse doesn't mind me staying late on Tuesdays to ensure the Campaign Objective.

Positive by Products worksheet
∗∗∗

Positive by Product:

Existing Benefit:	
Sabotaging by-product:	
Resolution:	
Resolution double check:	
Context double check:	

Positive by Product:

Existing Benefit:	
Sabotaging by-product:	
Resolution:	
Resolution double check:	
Context double check:	

Step 8

1. State the End Result in POSITIVE terms
2. Make sure the End Result is COMPLETELY within your control
3. Write it down as SPECIFIC as possible
4. List (using all 5 senses) the EVIDENCE for completion
5. Consider the CONTEXT
6. Assess the RESOURCES required
7. Consider the BY-PRODUCTS of changed actions
8. **Check the outcome's RIPPLE EFFECTS on the rest of your world**

Taking into account the effect of any change that is made (intentionally) that will (unintentionally)... on the wider systems of which a person is a part. Ecology is about the consequences for the system as a whole. Much of the American system champions our ability to keep our system separate from each other - which would be wonderful if it were possible. Ripple effects cause a great amount of confusion when entire systems come crashing down - because the ground rippled until the foundation crumbled.

It's also important to take into consideration how the campaign end result will effect and inform who you are as a person and what is important to you.

This step is easiest to appreciate if all the parts of your life (and the lives that your life touches) are viewed as a chess game. In chess you arrange your pieces on the board and when you are set up, you strike. Life does not require a zero sum solution; victor and defeated foe basis (as is in chess). However, everything you do (even if you're convinced it's wholly separate) has a ripple effect on those who you encounter. The more you encounter them, the more your decisions, choices, and outcomes will make the fluidity of their systems fluctuate.

There are four primary questions that allow consideration for the ripple effects of new outcomes:

1. What **will** happen if the outcome **is** achieved?

_____

2. What **won't** happen if the outcome **is** achieved?

_____

3. What **will** happen if the outcome **is not** achieved?

_____

4. What **won't** happen if the outcome **is not** achieved?

_____

It is important to answer this in consideration of those that are a part of the context of the outcome. (worksheet on next page)

First, answer these questions for yourself
Second, answer them for those you listed in chart 2 of the context worksheet (Step 5)
  o Many times, the ease of completion is increased when the objective's consequences are clearly articulated to those involved.
Third, answer, finally, for entities that are touched by you. (companies, venues and organizations)

Ripple Effects worksheet ***

Name being considered: _____

What **will** happen if the outcome **is** achieved?	
What **won't** happen if the outcome **is** achieved?	
What **will** happen if the outcome **is not** achieved?	
What won't happen if the outcome **is not** achieved?	

Name being considered: _____

What **will** happen if the outcome **is** achieved?	
What **won't** happen if the outcome **is** achieved?	
What **will** happen if the outcome **is not** achieved?	
What won't happen if the outcome **is not** achieved?	

Step 9

1. State the End Result in POSITIVE terms
2. Make sure the End Result is COMPLETELY within your control
3. Write it down as SPECIFIC as possible
4. List (using all 5 senses) the EVIDENCE for completion
5. Consider the CONTEXT
6. Assess the RESOURCES required
7. Consider the BY-PRODUCTS of changed actions
8. Check the outcome's RIPPLE EFFECTS on the rest of your world
9. **Write out CLARIFYING QUESTIONS for the 1st Step**

Defining the first step is vital to a well formed process. Clarifying questions are: Who, What, Where, When, Why and How. The form on this page is for the first step of the end result or outcome:

Who:

_____

What:

_____

When:

_____

Where:

_____

Why:

_____

How:

_____

RECORD THESE TASKS IN YOUR TASK LIST

Step 10

1. State the End Result in POSITIVE terms
2. Make sure the End Result is COMPLETELY within your control
3. Write it down as SPECIFIC as possible
4. List (using all 5 senses) the EVIDENCE for completion
5. Consider the CONTEXT
6. Assess the RESOURCES required
7. Consider the BY-PRODUCTS of changed actions
8. Check the outcome's RIPPLE EFFECTS on the rest of your world
9. Write out CLARIFYING QUESTIONS for the 1st Step
10. **Write down the NEXT outcome you will be allowed to do once this is complete**

Even though it is important to not get sidetracked in the process of an outcome - it is necessary to know that what you are working on is not eternal.

Write Down the Objective you are going to achieve NEXT. What is on the horizon?

- Don't get stuck thinking of this outcome as anything but a fun horizon.
    - You need to see the end as the result you want to see achieved.
- The end result or objective is what gives purpose and focus to your marketing and sales actions.

Farming: activity that pays off like planting seed in the fall to eat food next summer

1. **Keywords: the starting point**
2. **On-page/Off-page Optimization**
3. **Analyze and Adjust (seasonal)**

Social and SEO Overview

S.E.O. represents "Search Engine Optimization"
(instructions in step 2)

This section is a combination of the foundations of SEO (like: "THE PERIODIC TABLE OF SEO SUCCESS" chart from SearchEngineLand.com), and Farming work that you personally can do best, because it is based on you living your life in the connected world... today.

This is the first of (hopefully) many requests that you hire someone to do this. The only constant in today's booming technology mushroom cloud - is the fact that we still (usually) spell the word the same way each time it's used. The elements aren't even solidified enough for the ground to be walked on. It takes a team to keep up with the best ways to use these tools.

Here's one of my old element charts:

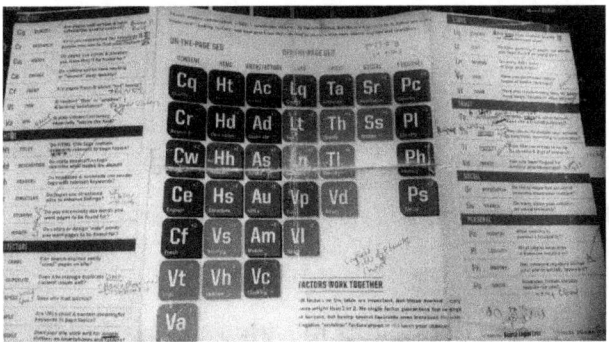

Base Everything on Value

Lack of communicating value provokes buyers to think that they can get what you sell from a number of other vendors, locations, or websites. It doesn't matter if it's accurate or not... if the buyer thinks it - it's a reality in the only mind that matters. The marketplace belief is that everything is a commodity or it's a new invention... and then it will be a commodity in 6 months. Bells and whistles are fine ways to distinguish yourself (to emotionally stimulate the buyer), but **if you're aiming at setting yourself apart based solely on features, advantages, and benefits; the only way to consistently earn business is to drop your price.** This always-accessible-cyber-resource destroys the number one bells and whistles selling tactic... the misconception that "information is exclusive". Value is worth buying, so it will still sell when the buyer does their research.

Pay Attention. (period)

People place a high value on insightful advice. If you're the one who understands what they *really* need (and are asking), you can sell what is an inferior product or service - based solely on the fact that you're the only one who can speak to what is foundationally on the buyer's mind.

Give value and track your expertise. Know the people who follow and listen to you. Touch base with them on a scheduled basis.

They are your referral partners and may even be your next lead.

Global Issue: Who do we trust?

A sad side note of our reality is that politicians and religious leaders aren't in the top 10 trustworthy positions held, whereas corporate experts are rated the second most valued opinion (next to an academic expert).

The primary difference is: When dealing with a corporate expert, it is understood that they're looking out for their own good, whereas political and religious leaders are thought to be (and claim to be driven) for the good of others, when it is clear that they are their only agenda. (typically)

This incongruence makes their opinion and influence lose its value when clear self-interest is trusted. It seems broken and backwards, but it's true.

Computer Work: Communicate Expertise

There are hundreds of channels to communicate expertise. Two samples are: 1) Your own page where you create content on an ongoing basis, and 2) An expertise Q&A platform.

Q&A forum:

If you're using a Q&A forum, look for a question that your target client would be asking and answer it. As you search past answers that are posted you may quickly begin to realize that many of the people who proclaim expertise need to stand corrected. Be nice when you disagree—experts don't need to argue... they just know.

Your own page:

Add one piece of expert advice that your clients could benefit from knowing. Think through your past month and answer one question or address one issue that you (as the value adding expert) know the answer to. Schedule a time tomorrow to do this again.

1. Keywords: the starting point

The core to build from is: <u>keywords</u>

At its source; the internet is still running a bunch of on/off switches (binary). Search Engines today use assumptive search algorithms, and if you **know (and use) the key words and phrases** that people have been searching for (based on the actual internet history of usage); there's a good chance some of those people will search for those words again; and when they do... search engines will think that some of the people who are searching (for those keyword terms) - are looking for you. *It works (despite design confusion) because of economy of scale.*

<u>Use two paths to come up with your Keyword list</u>

1. **<u>Human</u>: Think up the words that you would use to search.** (worksheets follow)

2. **<u>Computer</u>: View the actual phrases that are being searched.** (guide also follows)

<u>Define: Website Authority (aka. Link Juice)</u>

Website Authority: the authority that search engines give to a link, because it is coming from a website that internet history shows to be considered an authority on a certain topic. EXERCISES: Use keywords each time you create a link back to your website or social media (preferably from a website with authority).

<u>Here are the pieces of the Website Authority mechanism:</u>

- Search engines count each link on the internet as a vote (for the website the link opens)

- Some websites (of course) have more authority/clout/juice/powerful ranking authority given to their content than other sites

- The more authority the page with the link has (on the topic), the more credits/rank/position the search engines will give to the website on the other side of a link

- If you are able to connect the primary keywords for the:
  - Pages with the link
  - The text in the link, and
  - The page opened up when you click the link... it's a trifecta (that's a good thing)

Computer Work: How do you find those keywords?

There are many companies and websites that are devoted specifically to keyword selection. You can hire someone to build a list, or run a search for keyword selection websites and tools. *Select a list based on: topic, like minded websites, or industries that you are targeting. Two to three words in length with little competition and lots of local searches are great keywords to start using.*

Start with a quick brainstorming session:

List the top phrases that you would use to search for your business...

_____   _____

_____   _____

_____   _____

_____   _____

_____   _____

_____   _____

Keyword Creation worksheet

Pick a specific product or service; what would people search if they were buying your widget:

_____   _____

_____   _____

_____   _____

_____   _____

Pick your most respected competitor; what would people search if they were looking for them:

_____   _____

_____   _____

_____   _____

_____   _____

Considering the pain your business resolves (why people give you money); what would people search if they were looking to have that pain remedied:

_____   _____

_____   _____

_____   _____

Pick the top words from the previous page and look them up on thesaurus.com; what synonyms (or search word ideas) come from reviewing those words:

_____   _____

_____   _____

_____   _____

_____   _____

_____   _____

Think of the slang that people use when referencing your industry; what might people search:

_____   _____

_____   _____

_____   _____

Pull ideas off Google Keyword Generator

The best free tool at this point is from Google:
https://adwords.google.com/KeywordPlanner
- Log in
- Click "Tools" and then "Keyword Planner"
- There are three options to choose from, under the "find new keywords" header - these are not options. *These are **3 steps to a new keyword list**. Complete all of them.*
    1. **Search by Phrase, Website or Category**
    2. **Filter the list**
    3. **Add search terms that have been searched recently (that I didn't think of)**

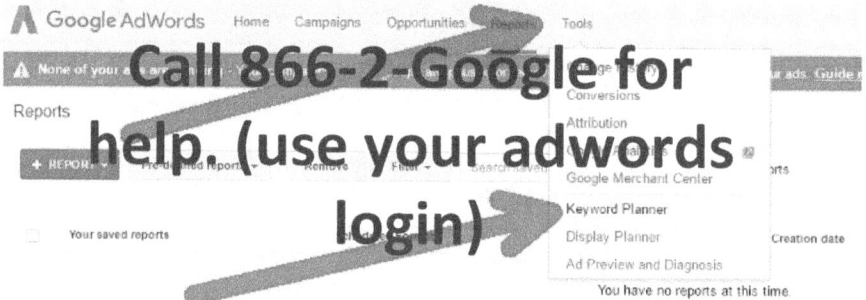

3 steps to a new keyword list. (in Keyword Planner click the "?" to define each piece)

1. Search by Phrase, Website or Category
Name used by Google "Search for new keywords using a phrase, website or category"
- Once you have the list created - download the list (select all & click download button)

2. Filter the list
Name used by Google "Get search volume data and trends"
- Upload the file you just downloaded (option 2)
- Use the filter "negative keywords". These are the words that you want filtered out. EXAMPLE: if you add "free"

to a search phrase as a negative search keyword, you're telling the search engine that you don't want keywords for people who are searching for "free"
- Once you have the list created - download the list (select all & click download button)

3. **Add search terms that have been searched recently (that I didn't think of)** This is a little tricky;
   Name used by Google "Multiple keyword lists to get new keywords"
   - Add the keywords that you downloaded in one of the boxes (copy/paste and edit)
   - Add the keywords that you created using the "Keyword Creation worksheet" in a box
   - Add negative keywords/targeting.
   - Once you have the list created - download the list (select all & click download button)

Keyword Planner instructions available at:
https://support.google.com/adwords/answer/3114286
Google help center homepage:
https://support.google.com/partners#topic=3110975

Example of a working keyword list

Keyword (by relevance)	Avg. monthly searches	Competition	Avg. CPC	Ad impr. share	
bing	13,600,000	Low	$0.21	0%	ACCOUNT
adwords	1,830,000	Low	$0.26	0%	ACCOUNT
adsense	1,830,000	Low	$0.05	0%	ACCOUNT
google adwords	1,000,000	Low	$0.29	0%	ACCOUNT
bing translator	673,000	Low	$1.42	0%	ACCOUNT
google adsense	673,000	Low	$0.05	0%	ACCOUNT
entrepreneur	368,000	Low	$1.08	0%	ACCOUNT
ads	246,000	Low	$0.87	0%	ACCOUNT
social network	165,000	Low	$1.23	0%	ACCOUNT

THIS AND OTHER KEYWORD TOOLS TELL YOU WHERE YOU START... DON'T "PUT THE CART BEFORE THE HORSE" ... GET YOU LIST OF KEYWORDS AND USE THEM.

2. On Page/Off Page SEO

Optimize your site, page or profile in order for Search Engines to recommend you. (this is S.E.O.)

1. On-page Search Engine Optimization

On-page optimization is what you do *to your* site, *to your* social media page, or *to your* directory listing.

- Make sure your name, industry and correct contact information is visible, up to date and correctly spelled. Be sure those words are on your page (and not just a picture of those words) ... text and not an image.

- Any image added to your page needs keyword based names, because "1574.jpeg" tells the search engines that that picture should show up when someone searches "1574". Naming your images is the first half. You can further aid search engines to understand what an image is about with an **"Alt tag"**. These two combine to help describe what a picture "looks like" to computers that can't see anything other than 1's and 0's.

- **Meta tags, meta titles, and meta descriptions** also help your site to be categorically understood.

  - A simple explanation of when you see these; anytime you run an internet search; there are multiple result options for you to select from. This is a "Search Engine Results Page".

- Your **meta title** is the headline that shows up (typically in blue text)

- the **meta description** is the sentence or two that shows up as a description of the meta title.

- **Meta Tags** are a list of keywords that are associated with that page. Most web creation platforms have a place to add "tags" to the page. These **"tags"** also group blog posts, pages, or media for visitors to find when they search your website.

- **Create great content. This is the final point in the overview of On-Page Optimization; and it is the most important.**

  ○ It doesn't matter how many people visit your page... if there's nothing legitimate for them to digest once they are there. Make your content something that real people want to look at, read, and come back to. Search engines like that. Don't stuff a page with keywords. If it's more than 5-10%, you're going to read like a bad used car commercial, "come down, dealer name, catch phrase" on repeat for 30 seconds... it's annoying... and people don't like it. Besides, if you get blacklisted by search engines, you won't show up anywhere—even when people are specifically looking for you and search your domain. Just write like you are talking face to face.

Quick overview for formatting your content:

A. **Header or Title**: This is what people read when your page is shared. Make it attractively descriptive. Use a good hook in the title (with the priority keyword for that page/post) to make viewers want to click on it when the search engine list appears.

B. **Bold and Hyperlink Text from the referring site**: If you have a link made up of the words, "Click Here" you are telling the search engines that the link (which is a vote) is about the phrase "click here". Make the keywords for which you are competing **bold** and hyperlinked.

C. **Organize the 'flow' of your site with named pages**. If the name of your page is P123, that doesn't tell the computers anything about that page, and it is confusing when shared. Name the page with a keyword, and make sure you're helping the search engines categorize what you are about.

For Instance: Digital and Physical Storefronts

Adjust perspective; make sure that you are aware of how people are using your pages.

If you noticed people walk into your retail store and each time they walk over to a particular display they immediately left your store; you would go over to that display, investigate it and maybe even ask people why they left, and then you would change the display.

Do the same thing with your website and other trackable pages, because this is one of the core benefits of Google Analytics.

2. Off-page Search Engine Optimization

Off-page optimization is what happens *on other* websites and pages with *links that point to you*.

- **Register on directories and social networks**. The initial step with directories is to recognize what listings are already set up in your name. As previously articulated, make sure your site has your exact contact information, because you want your other listings to reflect the same contact information (easier for computers to tie you to the map programs we all use). The point is to get business. Listings on directories, social media, Q&A forms, etc... help you to be found.

- **Other websites and blogs and event sites.** External links to a page or website hold the same formatting rules as on-page optimization links.

  - Any external site that has a link to your page. Hopefully that site is authoritative in your industry. **It should have links that are made up of *a keyword or phrase (preferably words that are the same primary keyword of the page that is being linked to)*.**

  - When you click the keywords; it opens (or links) to your site, social media or directory listing.

    - Every time someone clicks, there is a connection that the search engines make a note of.

  - Next time someone searches that keyword; the search engines may recommend you a little higher.

    - This is why we track website analytics. If the people who visit that page show (through analytics) to have found what they were looking for (on your website/page), your stock rises on future searches.

Whenever someone is looking for an answer, there is one place they go—the Internet.

In order to be found, there is a basic requirement: to create some type of content (picture/page/website/email/etc.) from which new clients will be able to find you.

Almost every piece of this chapter is based on using a computer and creating content as a marketing channel. Each of the "streams" listed are potential streams of income. You can consider them marketing campaigns, or sales 'lines in the water'.

Any of these tools you have *not set up yet* are potential lead generating channels without anyone working the field ...how can a crop grow where no work has taken place?

Set up what makes sense now. Do the work once and bookmark it (save it as a favorite), and you'll be able to add to it later, when you like.

Google: updates and rollouts

Google algorithms (like all search engines) are trying to keep ahead of users who try and manipulate the results for money. It's not always money, but it's usually money.

When there is a change in the standard process with which results are delivered, Google sometimes lets people know before, sometimes will confirm is afterward, and sometimes doesn't address it.

Past Google Search Updates that are worth knowing about:

- ## 2011
    - **"Panda"** update... you'll lose rank if:
        - **You have poor content**
          If you fix everything, you can regain position when the next Panda update is released by Google

- ## 2012
    - **"Top Heavy"** update... you'll lose rank if:
        - **You have too much advertising bling on your site (don't be all cleavage)**
    - **"Penguin"** update... you'll lose rank if:
        - **You have paid for links to trick Google (they don't like that)**
          If you are penalized by this, you can use Google Disavow Tool and the next time a Penguin update is released, you may regain your position
    - **"Pirate"** update... you'll lose rank if:
        - **You have copyright infringements registered with Google**
          This is probably a good place to mention that you can report copyright infringements to Google or most

companies that care about others copying what they own illegally

- ## 2014
    - ○ **"Pigeon"** update... you'll lose rank if:
        - • **You don't have a real local web presence across multiple networks and directories**
          This was Google's update to add Distance and Location Ranking Parameters to the search results (making way for mobile)

- ## 2015
    - ○ **"Mobile-Friendly"** update... you'll lose rank if:
        - • **Your website is not mobile friendly**
          This is where Google becomes the new (but free) version of business search (what we previously used the Yellow Pages for) ... map, info, call together on one screen.

Now; Format your Mobile for Local

Smartphones and tablets are the only computers many people use.

Mobile computing is here to stay.

- Mobile requires your page to be quick and light
- Local requires your page to be well connected

How do you address this?

- Make sure your website shows up properly formatted for a smart phone by looking at it and clicking through it.

- Make sure that your pages (and your content) is direct and succinct enough to be processed on the fly.

  - Preferably, you can set up alternate formatting for mobile viewers.

  - A benefit of mobile design is that you have less information and must assume that the visitor only has a few seconds. This is a great exercise to force yourself to communicate the main point accurately.

3. Analyze and Adjust (seasonal)

Be Where your Target Client is Looking

Existing paradox: You have future clients who are currently looking for you. They have not found you yet; but they will give you money - as soon as you can be found... **as long you as you show up where they're looking**. The tools that are in use today can have multiple purposes. There are **social networks** that can function as **blogs** and **directories** that can work as **websites** or **landing pages**, with every combination between. There's no set recipe.

Here are some income crops
****

Websites This is like a press packet for your company.
- **Your Blog(s)** Functions like an expert's journal/column
- **Landing Page** A brochure for specific item or event
- **Social Media Page** A business page on social media

Groups Affinity based online meeting for discussion
- **Social Media** Connect, hang out & chat (1on1 or groups)
- **Q&A's** Answer posted questions. It will rate expertise.
- **Forums** Groups that add input around specific questions

Email & Text Electronic newsletters sent to focus groups
- **Lists** Grouping contacts for targeted communication
- **Signature** Electronic business card with every message

Alerts & RSS Notification of other's content being published
- **Social Networks** Set notifications of certain type of activity
- **Target/Referral interest's Blogs** Track to give input
- **Industry Expert** Stay up on your industry competition

Listings Combined phone book, newspaper & magazine lists

- **Directories** Phone books, industry listings and reviews
- **Classifieds** Search or place want ads and local listings

Call Center: inbound and outbound calls (everything costs time or money)

- Surveys are still allowed by the Do Not Call list
- Processing inbound calls can save 100's of hours a year

CRM Customer Relationship Management (or Marketing)

- This can be paper or web based, but if you can't track when and why to follow up you've lost already.

Income Crops - a list of options

Income crops are: whatever you do to grow unsolicited income.

There are Income Crop ideas listed below; but anything that you do (or don't do) in order to create leads or income... is an income crop (and should be purposeful and based on the results that particular income crop is budgeted to create). **Each of the following crops of income will create leads, money, and referrals... be sure to analyze each month and adjust.**

Define: "Content" (so the following makes sense)

Any post, picture, video, documents, slideshows or even comments... whatever information you post or share... this is content. Each of these pieces of "Content" function like "seeds in the ground" when farming for business (3 fields are better than 1).

We spend our days creating content (emails, files, media, etc.). **Don't waste the next great piece of content you create - just change the names and share** with links that users/visitors/network would click back to your page. Content is everything that is sharable while looking at a screen.

Crop One, be an expert.

The reason you want to be seen as an expert is; so that referral partners or potential clients will find you when they're looking for expert information.

Implementation ideas & which **Content Channels** to use:
- **Website**:
    - Share your best articles as links on your site.
- **Your Blog(s)**:
    - Use all the content you create as opinions for future blog posts.

- **Landing Page**:
  - If you speak as an expert, create a landing page for the event to pack the house.
- **Social Media Page**:
  - Treat the build up like radio spots where you post the event & invite with a countdown to your network.
- **Q&A's**:
  - Find the questions that a target client would ask, and make sure you write or vote for the best answer.
- **Email & Text**:
  - Use the content posted elsewhere for newsletter content and include a link for people to see your reach.
- **Message Signature**: If you become established as an expert on a certain page or forum, include it in your email signature - more people see your email signature than any other piece of content (usually).

It is great to have people listen to what you have to say, but if there's no process to follow up and no clients are created—you've lost. Show your expertise now, so that when that future client is looking for information, you're one of the voices that they will find, and when they see that you know what you're talking about—they will contact you—if your contact information is available.

Crop Two, create content and distribute it.

Content can be a personal e-mail that is one sentence long and appears to be going out individually (but is actually customized to each person through "variable data"), or it can be as complex as an e-book that is written to be purchased as a download with its own website and Pay Per Click campaigns. Make it something you'd want to read and there is a good chance that others will be glad that they read it as well.

Implementation ideas & which **Content Channels** to use:

- **Websites** & **Your Blog(s)** & **Landing Page**:
  - There is very little (if any) content that you create that should not be available on your website and blog. Creating multiple posts can take time, but the reach can pay out for years. If you create a digital file and save it— you can be provided an email every time someone wants to download the eBook.
- **Social Media Page**:
  - Whenever you create solid content, share a link (with customized heading) on each of your social media pages.
- **Groups** & **Q&A's** & **Forums**:
  - When your answer to a public Q&A forum is based on a post or e-book you have previously written, share the link and direct readers to your page or e-book for a more detailed answer. It's even better if you can have someone else link their expert answer to your book or post.
- **Lists**:
  - Create content that fits a specific contact list and forward it with a short personal note and a link.
- **Directories**:
  - Whichever content gets the most traffic should be what is shared on the directories you use. If people like a piece of content on one social media network, there's a good chance people on another social media network will like it as well (because they're both following you).
- **Classifieds**:
  - If people love what you have created, offer it as an inexpensive product for a small fee. This is a great way to get paid to create proposals for larger future clients, while you are able to filter out the clients with whom you are not a great fit.
- **CRM**:

- All content is created in order to gather people's contact information. Create pre-written email response forms, and when you enter a business card into your CRM/contact list—send a quick follow up message asking them to follow you and thank them for their time when you met. Create the content and follow up on any response.

Crop Three, comment and engage other's content.

If you are reading the same article, listening to the same audio, or watching the same video... there's a good chance you have something in common. If you're someone who loves kid videos, someone who likes watching kid videos is a good target client (because you'd enjoy spending time with someone who likes the same types of videos that you do). Once you have taken the time to watch, read or listen to something, take the time to comment on what you like, because it may lead to a conversation... which may lead to a connection and possibly to a lead or referral partner. **Get to know people who are engaging in the same stuff you are.**

A Couple of points to keep in mind:

- Set your profile to be notified of comments on the same page or post you have engaged—they are people who have similar interests. **People like people who are like them.** It's a strong possibility that their friends are similar to you and your friends, which makes relationally connecting with them (to the point of passing referrals your way) a high likelihood.

- Don't get caught being negative online. If this is a possible lead generation source—you don't want to attract people who are drawn to complaint, because they will carry those same tendencies to everything else they do (including your business).

Implementation ideas & which **Content Channels** to use:

- **Social Media Page**:
  - As you find content on social media that is applicable to your business; sharing or reposting them on your business page is a great way to make connection with the author, as well as adding content that didn't require your time to create it.
- **Groups**:
  - The point for online or in person groups is to be social. If you're a part of a group, engage or it's no more beneficial to your business than watching TV or reading a newspaper.
- **Q&A's & Forums**:
  - Most forums and discussion boards list questions that haven't been answered or closed separate. Find that list and start your process of being the expert in your field.
- **Lists**:
  - If and when you give an answer that you are particularly proud of, include it in your next email marketing or text marketing distribution.
- **Alerts & RSS & Social Networks & Classifieds**:
  - Find the words that your target clients use. Set up alerts to be notified when they show up on blogs, social media, or anywhere else. Eventually you will be able to come up with some pre-fabricated responses to certain posts that may turn into a business conversation. Be sure you don't sound too business-y because you'll be ignored.

Crop Four, set up Search Alerts.

Be notified when topics that relate to you are to be engaged online with an offer to connect one on one to pitch them, or just answer some questions. Start being the available expert.

Implementation ideas & which **Content Channels** to use:

- **Groups & Social Media**:

- If you have a potential client that you're trying to get in front of; there should not be anything that they put on social media, a blog or website content that you are not aware of - and respond to (when appropriate).

- **Forums:**
  - See if there are any blogs creating content but not following up on the questions submitted. Many of these questions are buying signals that you can poach. You don't have to read every blog to "pay attention" to them—just be notified when someone adds a comment and glance at each notification.

- **Email & Text:**
  - When you notice a post of an issue/problem (that could be related to your industry expertise);
    - send an email (that may appear to be mass produced) that will happen to address the exact issue that they currently have.
    - Followed up with an interest call or personal (short text only) email to open doors.

- **Lists:**
  - Have everything that your "big fish" or "whale" (the largest potential clients... who could change your business) posts on the web tracked to notify you at least daily - know their company better than their employees.

- **Alerts & RSS:**
  - Have alerts sent to your e-mail once a day (or as they happen) for specific keywords using Google Alerts (www.google.com/alerts)

- **CRM:**
  - Any post by a potential client could turn into a lead down the road. It should be placed in your CRM with a

reminder set for when to get back and reach out the potential client.

Crop Five, the web is social, so engage.

Social media, forums, groups, and even Q&As are simply groups that function like any other community organization—the biggest difference is that these groups are available when it's best for your schedule. Find groups that will give referrals (or pick groups that may include potential clients). You're not doing this for fun (even though you should enjoy the content you're creating and socializing around). Find the groups that will provide income or referrals, and stop in once in a while—digitally.

Implementation ideas & which **Content Channels** to use:

- **Website** & **Your Blog(s)**:
  - o Whenever it fits, be willing to provide your website or a link to content that includes your contact information.
- **Social Media Page**:
  - o If you're on a social network for your business, be sure that you are using the social network AS YOUR BUSINESS. Some social networks allow you to be logged in as a business or as yourself—be the one you're functioning as. Don't make all your contact points be based on your personal profile, because your friends don't want to always remember you asking them for money (which is business). This is one of the reasons you create a business page.
- **Groups**:
  - o Online groups are the same thing as in person groups, so if you find discussions that could lead to business—go back there and meet more people.
- **Social Networks**:

- Friends aren't usually sources for business, but they are great sources for referrals (as long as you don't ask too often). Most friends are more than willing to help you - as long as you don't ask. Just present the opportunity and see if they can make the connection. Whenever a client says something nice to you directly - that's a great time to ask them for a referral.

- **Q&A's & Forums**:
  - Find some questions that apply to your industry which have been answered by professionals in a similar (but not exact industries) and meet that person (who is an expert in that similar industry). Look for connections who may be a referral partner (both directions). There are many industries that are so niche oriented, that experts in one area would LOVE to have someone in similar area to whom they could refer business (especially if that referral partner paid them for referrals).

- **Email, Text & Lists**:
  - If there's a potential lead that just doesn't work out, but likes your expertise; ask them if they'd like to be on an email or text list. It's hard to say no to a 1 on 1 ask.

- **Industry Listings, Directories & Classifieds**:
  - As you find potential referral partners, pay attention to where they show up (when you search them). These may be great locations for you to set up a listing or public profile with links to your different web presence pages and sites.

Crop Six, publicize your phone, email and domain where people search.

Directories are the new yellow pages. Even though many parts of the sales cycle can be automated, there comes a point when most people like to connect with another human before spending money. Clients look you up on their favorite directly and call.

Implementation ideas & which **Content Channels** to use:

- **Website, Your Blog(s)** & **Landing Page**:
  - o Every page on your site should have your contact info. This isn't a game of hide and seek—let them find you.
- **Social Media Page, Groups, Social Media, Q&A's** & **Forums**:
  - o Fill out profiles as complete as possible. Be certain your contact information is accurate. Don't be in a hurry and mistype your email or any other piece of contact info (it confuses the computers running the search engines).
- **Signature**:
  - o Don't have your contact info be too small, a light color, or as a part of a picture. Most emails don't download the images without an extra mouse click. When I can't find someone's contact info - I always go back to their email first (make it easy to connect with you).

Analyze and Adjust (recap)

A system is only as good as the person running it.

Make sure you use some kind of analytic software and track:

- Which pages site visitors first land on.
- Where they're spending the most time.
- Where they're leaving.
- What pages they came from last to go to your site.
- Where they're going from yours.
- https://support.google.com/analytics/answer/4553001

If you find a link on your blog post that directs to a competitor (or an old vendor) - remove it. If 80% of the people who read that blog post click on that link and leave your website; change that link to open a purchase now page on your site, or a comparison page that shows your superiority - or just delete the link ...but know what's happening in your own digital storefront. This is your business you're talking about - manage it well. *(if you're not sure how to do the above, that's OK... as long as you are using a vendor who can)*

Rule of Thumb: Computers are People

One of the biggest web marketing issues (and interpersonal communication issues) today is that we treat virtual communication as if the people on the other end don't receive the communication with the same power and force as if we were standing in front of them.

Instead; truth would have us treat the "computer" (and everyone who we "speak with" through the screen portals) as a real person (because they are). The problem with this effort is; even if we give effort to treating each comment in the same way we would if we were standing face to face... we won't have the response information. We will not see the look on their face, whether our statement makes them smile a little or makes their eyes sad. Text only communication is a painfully stunted form of communication, but it is the primary point of communication today - so figure it out, learn from your errors... analyze and adjust.

Treat your "Computer" message like it's a person, because there is a real live human on the other side of that screen - there's just a slight time delay.

Fishing: activity that catches a big one, but takes time to understand the target

1. **Select Location**
   - (Choose which Hole to fish today)

2. **Create and Distribute Content**
   - (Choose the Bait to use)

3. **Turn Traffic into Real People**
   - (The Cast)

4. **Socially Engage People**
   - (Set the Hook)

5. **Analyze and Adjust moment by moment**
   - (Fish in Net)

1. **Select Location** (Choose which Hole to fish today)

The purpose for fishing for business is the same purpose as farming for business or hunting for business; to get more business. New business starts with a new introduction - that new introduction is what you're fishing for.

<u>New connections come through an introduction:</u>

1. Request from visitor (This is "farming" for business)

2. Introduction ("you should meet..." is from "fishing")

3. Pitch as a vendor (overview in the next "hunting" section)

<u>**Introductions Close.**</u>
GET REFERRALS!!!
(all the time)

Referrals are the commodity of our age... don't ignore them (always respond). Certainly don't be afraid to ask for them.

Three easy steps to pick up reviews:
1. Listen for people to give you a complement
2. Ask if they'd be willing to give a 5-star review regarding that on social media (wait for an answer)
3. You keep your name/personal brand in front of your referral network through "content"

Two tools in referral generation:

Give to get endorsements

- The web is designed for endorsements, referrals, opinions and recommendations; so pass out some praise. Give a review; then be willing to ask them if they would endorse you back.

Implementation ideas & which **Content Channels** to use:
- **Website** & **Your Blog(s)**: Create a place on your website or blog where your endorsements are stored (providing links there to your other branded pages). Remember; every link is a vote, an endorsement... telling search engines to recommend this page. **Social Networks, Industry Listings, Directories**: Once you give an endorsement, check their network for people they know who could be a lead. This will put you in their network, and expand your reach to their

friends. If you endorse your current clients (especially those who fit your target client description), your network will grow with people who are your target client description (by being exposed to their network). **Email & Text**: Newsletters are great places to offer positive words about a client, because everyone likes public praise. This also makes your marketing email less "ME-centric", while creating more links to and from your web presence.

Ask every new client where they found you

- Do this for every client and keep track of the answers! As you find a source that is delivering new clients that you enjoy— grow it. You're giving time and energy to design your pipeline and sales process around attracting your target client... so complete the cycle and find out where you are being found.

Implementation ideas & which **Content Channels** to use:
- **Your Blog(s)**: As you deduce that a certain source is generating leads, write a blog or two that is specifically targeted to this source - and share those blog posts on those source networks. **Landing Page**: If there are a significant number of leads that come from a specific site or directory, it may be a good idea to set up a landing page for visitors from that source. This will give a customized transition to your website; and that specific contact form can designate the source of the lead. **Social Media Page**: People who connect with your social media page may have been referred there by a friend or colleague, a posting or link. When the path to connect with you is exposed; you may uncover a source of raving fans that you didn't know about. **Signature**: If you are a referral based business, add a request for a "5-star review" to your email and text signature line (with a link). Keep is

simple. **Directories**: Some people will come across your listing and think of someone that could use you, but unless they have a valid reason (like receiving income or feeing security in giving a referral due to another positive review being posted); they may pass on your name.

Global Issue: Social Networks and Real Life

Our physical and digital worlds are becoming completely interconnected.

Digital Activity Statistics for Businesses:

- 7.5 out of 10 people do not look past the options ranked on the 1st page of web search results.

- Over half of the company pages on social media have no marketing plan for their page... and most of those have never created one piece of content. Companies take the time to set up an account, but never use the tool to acquire new prospects or develop existing clients.

- The biggest statistic of all is that half of your target clients who have a social network presence **used it yesterday**.

*** Target clients are already online ***

*** They are looking for information ***

The question is whether I am on the list of people that they will use, or if my competition is responding to their emails, direct messages, and comments.

I want to be the former.

What is the purpose of having a Network?

All the networking building in the world is never an end in itself. The point is to have the contacts to call when the time is right, so they could help you toward your desired end.

When you need something specific, or if you're just having a follow up meeting with someone you met at a networking event; the question you ask is:

- o **"WHO DO YOU KNOW THAT I COULD TALK TO THAT MIGHT BE ABLE TO HELP US OUT?"**

If you meet with anyone (whether they are possibly a prospect or not):

- o **"WHO DO YOU KNOW THAT I COULD TALK TO THAT MIGHT BE ABLE TO HELP US OUT?"**

If you have an event, you are starting to publicize:

- o **"WHO DO YOU KNOW THAT I COULD TALK TO THAT MIGHT BE ABLE TO HELP US OUT?"**

If you are looking for more sales:

"WHO DO YOU KNOW THAT I COULD TALK TO THAT MIGHT BE ABLE TO HELP US OUT?"

This is the business purpose for having a network. We're all here to help each other out. Your network can't help you attain your goal if you don't ever ask.

No matter the location you target, there are rules to follow

Five guidelines for group interaction:

1. **If you solicit business non-stop, you will be blacklisted.** Events are social, so be... social. People you meet aren't always the ones that buy from you. They are (many times) your brand translator, and introduce you to your next client. *Your name* will come to the top of their mind as they encounter someone looking for what you offer. If you're an annoying salesman who is always pitching and never listening—even when a potential referral partner thinks that you may be good fit... you're not worth the risk of making them look bad by mentioning your name to someone they know (no one likes annoying sales).

2. **When you're the listener, follow their story as if you lived it.** As you learn to pay attention to someone else speaking, there are a couple things that will take place. (1) You will realize people are drawn to you and want to have time with you listening to them - listening to others is an uncommonly powerful communication tool. (2) You will recognize when the person you're 'speaking' with has checked out (don't check out). If you're giving your time to use social encounters for business, be present and engaged— here and now until you're done with the conversation and dismiss yourself with grace.

3. **Have one niche in which you are the expert.** If your response to," What do you do?" is, "Well, I do this and that for money, but this other thing is really what I love to do, and..." ...you may as well have said that you're a philosopher and a CPA during an interview to be an astronaut. You *actually may* be all of those; but you're not going to be hired as an astronaut based of your philosophy degree and CPA clientele. **If your pitch is that you do multiple jobs, it means you aren't good enough to specialize in any of them.** It doesn't matter how many sources of income you have—only what specialty you pitch. Be the niche expert in one specific segment that you can confidently... be an expert. Give people a reason to feel good that they know you and give you money.

4. **Always be ready to give your contact info.** Share your contact information through social media, email signatures, and your profile/page; because it only takes a minute to get them set up, and is then automatically added to every communication that follows on that platform. For all planned and impromptu in-person connections, always have a business card - always. Business cards are quickly becoming the only remaining stationary for business—so use it to communicate your brand. Business people have business cards—don't make your job appear to be a hobby.

5. Finally, **have a hook**. This is something that will help people remember you, and is best when it references your expertise. You don't have to be a clown to be memorable. Have one thing (unique apparel, insightful phrase, cool collateral, etc.) that will cement you into their memory—in a good way.

2. Create and Distribute Content
(Choose the Bait to use)

There are two channels with which you can create and distribute content.

1. **A Campaign paid with money**

    a. Write ads/content

    b. Distribute by Paying Per Click

2. **A Campaign paid with time (Socially be your Personal Brand)**

    a. Join Group

    b. Social Media

    c. Attend Event

    d. Cold Call

    e. Referral

Share your content as many places as possible, but customize the content to fit the audience it is being shared with... and ask for a response.

The goal is to have specific individuals respond.

Your web presence can be your most direct point of contact with potential new clients, but the content you create cannot *only be* what you add to *your own* website. When you read a news story or industry blog post... don't hesitate to comment. You already took the time to read the article/watched the video/etc., and it's something that you are interested in... so there is a good chance that those who are going to read your comment will enjoy the same content you do. Make it well-written and positive; there is never an excuse for grammar mistakes or spelling errors or rude comments or non-business building words... remember your purpose.

Multiple Sources of Content

You're not the only one who can create content for your business. Often, you may be the least productive content creator anyway.

First step: ask your trusted clients and friends to give you a 5 Star Review. Have them do this from their own computers (and their own personal profile login).

Web reviews are based on an average. If you have five 5 Star Reviews and someone gives you a two star, your average will stay high. If you don't have any reviews and that same disgruntled customer gives the same 2-star review... it may take a while until you're close to a 4-5 star (by average). Use your network to have positive comments on your reviewable profiles.

It's much easier to recover from an irate zero review from someone who has a grudge if you have a few 100% praises... than it is for you to recover if you have a C and you get a zero.

Cold Calling Today

Direct Introduction (cold call or prospecting)

Those who think that cold calling or telemarketing or sales prospecting is a thing of the past... are the only ones who are handicapped by that belief. People who are using lead generation tools are benefiting from them (if the tools are being used correctly). Direct introductions grow out of meeting your targets where they currently spend time.

How do you "go where your clients currently spend time"

1. **Introductory Email from a mutual contact**
   a. There is no channel that insures the prospect will pick up your call more than a personal recommendation to speak with you (from someone who they currently trust)
2. **Group Attendance**
   a. They may not have anyone who does what you do - how you do it) i.e. networking, trade shows, through a screen via the internet, face to face, or direct chat
3. **Telemarketing**
   a. Have a lead list
   b. Call lead list with a specific question
4. **Be an Expert**
   a. Q&A forums for your industry
   b. Social Media Question (you answer)
5. **Send Surveys, Polls, Events and Giveaways (content)**
   a. Blogs with 20+ posts/month increase traffic from 55%-70%
   b. Email Marketing doesn't have to be a HTML newsletter (send a short personalized text)
6. **Comment and Engage Others that are reading the same stuff you are**

a. If you have taken the time to read something - respond and interact
b. Set to be notified of other comments & look 'ins'

7. **Google Alerts/Reader**
   a. Have alerts sent to your email inbox once a day/as they happen
   b. Track everything your potential lead posts to the web - go to a reader you look at daily
      i. See what's coming up. See if there's any blogs that are creating content. Is there a platform on which competitors are not following up on the questions that are clearly "buying signals" (defined in "Hunt" section under "Pipeline Responses"? This is a great way to poach "low hanging fruit"

8. **Get into Groups/Forums**
   a. These can be networking groups or community organizations (virtual or in person)
   b. Only involve yourself in enough groups so that you can engage & make contacts
      i. Find groups that will give referrals or be potential clients
      ii. You're not doing this for fun (even though it helps if you do things that you enjoy)

9. **Give and Get Endorsements**
   a. Google Places, Facebook, LinkedIn Endorsements... anywhere that's publicized
      i. Give the review/endorsement and then ask them to endorse you
      ii. This will put you in their network & expand your reach each time you connect

10. **Old Fashioned Classified Ads (great for product highlight or new location)**
    a. Craigslist is the standard at this point
       i. Write templates to use on a rotating basis.
       ii. Once you have written the template & receive a good response... why not use it again?

3. Turn Web Traffic into Real People by saying "hi" (The Cast)

Without a plan (or referral); the most difficult part to any business introduction... is the introduction.

APPROACH TECHNIQUES

Transitions from one approach to another must be smooth, logical, and convincing.

The basis for approaching a potential client today requires enough tact and courtesy to be able to approach them multiple times without turning the potential client off. Each of the approaches detailed and overviewed are options that are intended to use people's natural internal biological systems, and use those systems to work in the direction of the business we are approaching them to pitch.

- ## First Option... always; be Straight Forward and Direct
    - A direct approach is the best approach... always. There's nothing that's quite as powerful as a direct approach. There is trust that is placed on someone (down the road) if history has proven them to be an honest, straight forward person.
    - The Trouble with this approach: If the other person is being indirect, pieces of a direct approach would be negotiated in a false paradigm. It seems backwards; but in order to have a clear productive conversation (direct approach), you need to assess which type of indirect approach the other person is using to have a clear negotiation. Another reason to adjust from this approach is if the other person pulls away or shuts off. These responses can be symptoms of an issue the other person has with your proposal, or it could be a strategy used to give them the upper hand in negotiation.
    - Options:

- Engage their **Emotions**
- Give an **Incentive**

Tools to gauge your Target Client/Potential Lead's comfort with direct conversation:

- ## Leading questions
  - Setup the other person to be quick to offer an answer.
- ## Vague questions
  - Allow the other person to show you how much they know (whether you know the answer or not).
- ## Quick and Simple response questions
  - Designed to have them give a quick response when they see the question. If you're tracking the platform when they give the answer; there's a good chance that you can find yourself in a quick chat conversation (impromptu from the other person's perspective) that can double as a transition to the next step.
- ## Compound questions
  - This infers that you are in the process of research by asking a question with more than one specific answer. DO NOT PRETEND THAT YOU ARE GOING TO BE A CLIENT BY THE QUESTION YOU ASK. POSITION YOURSELF CORRECTLY FROM THE BEGINNING OF THE RELATIONSHIP, ASK AND LISTEN.
- ## Prepared questions
  - Every business and industry has questions that are designed to fester the pain in a potential client... in an effort to have them choose to make a change (in which they pay you for your product or service).
  - If you don't have a few of these written out, stop and write out at least one prepared question that you can ask someone who may be a good client. (pg. 25 ...in case you skipped it)

- ## EMOTIONAL APPROACHES
  - Emotions are chemicals that flow through our body. They are based on our view of ourselves; mixed with our relationships with others. If you pay attention and observe during the initial stages in conversation, look for:
  - Is their baseline emotion greed, love, hate, revenge, or another? Is he or she loving, hateful, just self-absorbed, all about the money, etc.? You have to know the baseline of the other person or you will never understand the variations that emerge.

    Question/Actions to recognize emotional variations during rapport building:
    - Are they inward or outward focused?
    - Connect on some life experience and apply pressure to see which emotions show up
    - If true; link the feeding of that emotional appetite with the business at hand

Even though emotions are the key hook when fishing for business, emotional pull is almost useless without an incentive.

- ## INCENTIVE APPROACH
  - To over-simplify this tool; you are offering something the other person wants in exchange for something you want. It's important that you never offer something you can't fulfill. Even when you can fulfill what you're committing to; anytime you pay with incentive for cooperation from the client, you forever step into the negotiation relationship. If you try and go back to the rapport building after offering incentive or reward as a basis to move forward; most intelligent humans will recognize that friends don't need to buy their friendship. Also, once you have gone to the incentive zone, there is a good chance the other person will begin to position

themselves to get some greater incentive - during the remainder of the negotiation (and business partnership).
Common Rewards:

- Free Introductory Service
- Gift Card
- Information
- Personal Gift within Business Negotiation
- Remove their pain (real or imaginary)

- ## **Selecting an Approach:**
  - o When there is not enough information to know what direction is best to move forward in the conversation; begin to run through a few questions that do not have anything to do with the specific step within the campaign, but do have to do with the client. Anything that has to do with the client is good background information to create a more informed proposal (in the long run).

  - o These questions include (but are not limited to):
  - o Asking about immediate past events with the other person or their business
    - This will inform the mindset of the other person, as well as giving insight as to which approach would be most productive.
  - o Asking background questions.
    - This includes asking about the source's family, work, friends, likes, and dislikes. These types of questions can develop rapport and provide clues as to the source's areas of knowledge or reveal possibilities for incentives or emotional approaches.
  - o Considering what are culturally and socially acceptable topics of discussion.
    - For example, asking one male about his wife could be considered extremely rude, whereas not asking an another the same question might be seen as insensitive.

- ## **Smooth Transitions**
  - o If the conversation continues in a direct approach, there is no need for transitioning between different

techniques/emotional processes listed below. However, when these approaches are beneficial; weave them together into an honest, logical thought pattern (that shows you have listened and understood where the other person is coming from). That is the point one of these indirect approaches during a campaign will allow the conversation to be brought into the direct path of your pitch... and you ask it directly, listen and close the sale.

- o Often, a wonderful transition tool for creating a smooth transition between two different approaches (while speaking face to face) is found in asking a seemingly unrelated question. Be careful to not abruptly jump off the track! The potential client is already thinking about multiple points (when deciding to give you business), the last thing the other person needs is a change in conversation that causes them to stop thinking about how much they would like to buy your product or service... to focus on an interpersonal conversation interruption.
- o Make transitions smooth. If you're not good at this, start practicing. Use an unrelated question and see if you can't use the following tools throughout the week.

Define: Subjective vs. Objective

1. Subjective: I'm personally the subject which assumes bias and individually influenced opinion.

2. Objective: I'm outside of the equation to the point I can see people, actions and factors as objects.

Sales Tip: Read Your Prospect

You cannot not communicate. *70% of communication is believed to be nonverbal.*

We all put out signals of our internal process... all day - every day. It is not only about perceived body language, eye movement or breathing patterns... reading people involves hearing the pace, pattern, and length of silence mixed with non-verbal cues (poker "tells"), and never firmly assuming their intent - just guessing. **Listen with an open hand.**

- *Example: **Where they look when you address cost.** If they glance at a picture of their family or play with a wedding ring every time price is mentioned, it could mean that they trust their spouse's opinion on these topics, or that they're gauging the effect of this decision on their family or kids (next vacation or birthday present). **All resources pull from somewhere else.** Consideration of family could reflect the pain that pulls them away from saying 'yes', or the pleasure that is drawing them toward saying 'yes'.*

Listen with all 5 senses.

Other Approaches to use and combine

Most of these tools are nothing more than emotional connections that are identified and classified. Use them in combination or stand alone, but always keep in mind the purpose for which you are in the conversation... business.

1. Calm Down Approach
    - **The Goal**: to be an outlet for the resolution of fear
      The Process:
    - Find an existing fear within the other person
    - Provide outlets and cushions for that fear
    - Describe concrete actions that he/she will take in order to remove the client's fear
2. Careful Critiques Approach
    - **The Goal**: push down on their ego (careful!), just enough to have the other person press to prove that he or she is worth being in this conversation; and will give valuable information to prove they are the worthy

- o **Example**: by critiquing a beautiful and vain girl about her looks (when it's certain everyone around her always complements her), you are causing her to press to win your approval, because that is the appetite that she is used to having fed by everyone she meets, but don't be a pig!
- o Tools:
  - Question if he/she is the actual decision maker
  - Question who else should be in the conversation
- o IT IS IMPORTANT; DON'T OFFEND, BUT MAKE SURE THE SIGNER IS SITTING AT THE TABLE OR YOU'RE RELYING ON THE SALES SKILLS OF THE PERSON YOU PRESENTING TO... TO SELL IT TO THE PERSON WHO SIGNS THE AGREEMENT

3. Connection with Fear Approach
   - o **The Goal**: to be an outlet for the emotion of fear
     The Process:
   - o Find an existing fear within the other person
   - o Link the existing fear to a resolution of your pitch

- o "It's Hopeless" Approach
  - o **The Goal**: remedy the frustration of a hopeless mess (probably solved by whatever you're selling).
  - o Tools: Use facts only. If someone is feeling helpless and starts to trust you... and then recognizes that you were not being truthful, your door to this client may be shut for good

- o Low Self Worth Approach
  - o **The Goal**: flatter the other person in an effort to have them instruct you on how to best sell them the product or service you're pitching (to them)
    The tools:
    - Acceptable complements and recognition of an area they like to see themselves as an expert
    - Obvious flattery will end the relationship and insult the other person - be careful
    - Speak highly of the other person or what they offer to the conversation
  - o Where this works: works well with someone who is underqualified, underappreciated or just has low self esteem
  - o Variation of this tool: this also works well on people with a strong ego. If you let their ego drive them to talk about how

smart they are to bring you on board... you will have them closing you (rather than the other way around)

- **New Location**
  - o **The Goal:** change the setting to reset the conversation (at a neutral location or public location) so the other person will be encouraged to stop whatever activity is creating an obstacle for the business at hand
  - o <u>When to use:</u>
    - To create increased comfort
    - To create discomfort (as a reset)
- **Positive Approach**
  - o **The Goal:** connect some positive emotion to a tangible end result - helping the sale
  - o The key to this approach (and any other approach of emotion) is in solidifying the tangible representation of this emotion. Pulling on an emotion is good, but knowing how that emotion connects to a real person or priority... is priceless
  - o Love (from brotherly love to intimate love) is a dominant emotion in most people. Communicate how your product or service feeds the emotion of love inside a potential client (and memorize the outline). If you're able to show how your product can benefit those loved by a potential client, all the better
- **Pain Approach**
  - o **The Goal:** identify and fester an unresolved pain to encourage action to fix it
  - o Sandler Sales Training Program was built on the concept of; Identify the pain, highlight the pain, and present a solution to the pain... because avoiding pain is a high priority for every potential client you will meet
  - o One of the great benefits to pain; when focused on, it has the ability to completely overshadow reason. It also can blind us to what we are missing in pursuit of the remedy of the pain being addressed
- **Quick Q&A session**
  - o **The Goal:** use a seamless Question and Answer session to position the other person as the power source for the conversation

- Tools to use:
  - Don't' always keep the questions going in the same direction. Once you get a link of questions going, change the topic every few questions to keep the other person giving effort to keep up with whatever line of questions that they are the expert on
  - This is good approach to use if you have two or more people on your side of the negotiation. This allows the potential client to "hold court" or be the giver of information and the feeling of power will often make them forget the pieces of information that they don't want to share... because it's so much fun to be the "Great and Powerful Oz", even if you're actually just a small man behind the curtain
  - Use the client's sensory words to make sure they know that you're tracking with them (as they are being the expert)
- Repetition
  - Some people in business are convinced that they know what you are going to say before you say it. These people are difficult to converse with, because they don't listen. Repetition is a good tool to use with this type of conversation
  - **The Goal:** repeat the question as many times as it takes to have the client become relaxed (and even bored) with the conversation to answer directly (whenever they actually hear the question).
- Silence
  - Silence is confusing to our culture. We are surrounded by noise and often don't have time to hear ourselves
  - When to Use:
    - Best used with an overly confident or overly nervous person
      - Look for fidgeting or nervous activity
      - Also look for aloof indifference (that shows confidence)
    - Gives an opportunity to let the other person's words hang in the air for a while before responding. Same premise works on text conversation. If you take a week

or two off between conversations, the client will be required (by human forgetfulness) to go back and read the previous messages (to catch up on what the negotiation was about) before responding. This silence will allow them to read /hear themselves (not that they will start listening, but maybe)

- We have all the information Approach
  - **The Goal:** communicate to the other person that you have reviewed all the information that they're wanting to check on before making a decision. To present that you have done the work and know that this is the best option for them to move forward
  - Preparation: If this is an approach that is used, it's absolutely vital that all relevant facts (for this case) are known by you. Don't get caught pretending like you have the answers they are looking for (but can't answer a simple question they have during the appointment)
  - Tools to Use:
    - Act a little bored (because from your perspective of expertise, you're explaining something that's actually quite simple)
    - It's in the Files (Approach in combination): If you have the time to prepare a file, any folder with paper inside it can communicate that you have done enough research to know more about the client than the client knows (but never say this)
    - Adding any tabs or sticky-notes hanging outside of the file adds a sense that the files aren't enough to hold what you have uncovered

Game: I know what you're up to

When I target someone; (before our meeting) I look them up to see what is available. If there is a reference to a certain part of the world or a favorite activity, I add the topic to our conversation to see if they will personally connect. ***Assumed similarities breed trust.***

On most social networks, I will know if they're a new parent or if their kids just went off to college. Every piece of information helps me know how to connect more effectively.

You have something in common with everyone— just find it.

Game: Truth or Liar

Try to gather a couple of pieces of information before you meet with anyone. In your initial conversation ask a couple questions that you know the answers to... along with a couple you don't. If the other person answers falsely or doesn't have any desire to connect personally - recognize their preference and build the rapport they prefer... just get down to business and move on.

The first gives their Truth Teller status and the second gives your information.

4. Socially Engage People (Set the Hook)

The Mechanics of Communication (since that's what we're doing)

Human communication is both chemical and mechanical.

It's an art *and* a science.

St. Francis de Sales said, "True progress quietly and persistently moves along without notice." That is how our development as communicators takes place; and every once in a while... it is vital to have a tune up and clear the cob webs out of our under-used communication engines... change the fluids that keep us moving in the right direction. This is not a task to be checked off when conquered, but a skill to develop throughout life. This section is designed to be a resource to understand what's actually happening when we talk.

****

Which of the 5 senses do you **use the most**, and which ones do you **never take notice of**?

- MOST VALUED IN OUR CULTURE: See, Hear & Touch (touch/feel is usually in a contrast with "thinking")
- LEAST USED: Taste and Smell.

1. Every communication factor is taken in through the five senses

External event is taken in through one or more of our sensory input channels

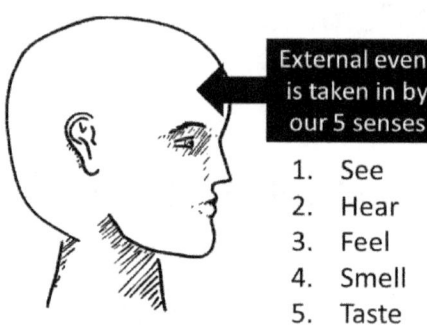

External event is taken in by our 5 senses

1. See
2. Hear
3. Feel
4. Smell
5. Taste

Those are the only channels through which these physical bodies can receive information. As you take in stimuli, understand its source and result. Even though most people have access to all five senses, it's important to clarify which are your favorites... and which are not. People who make decisions based on certain sensory channels will trust that they are being heard if you use the same sensory words; whereas conflicting sensory words may provoke them (or you) to be annoyed (or think less of the other person).

You may see that the type of communication the other person is using as silly and pointless.

- If you're a thinker (someone who values the rational data being fully processed before a decision is made), you may not have great respect for people who are feelers.

- If you're a feeler, a lot of times, you classify people who are thinkers as those who don't get the <u>real</u> big picture.

- Both decision making paradigms are valid to the person using them. Everyone else does what they do on purpose, and they're living their lives without the necessity of being more like you. Stick to what you're there to do.

We all have a justification for the channels, tools, and processes we use. The fact that I don't understand why the other person makes decisions using the tools they use—doesn't mean that there's not a valid reason for their decisions (even if they're dead wrong). What senses do you prefer to reference in communication?

* *
* *

As you take content in through your five senses, it...

2. Goes through our Filters.

System of Human Communication:

Our brain translates the signals from our sensory receivers through our unconscious filters

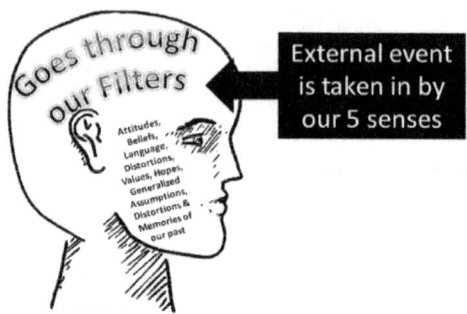

These filters are your <u>attitudes</u>, <u>beliefs</u>, <u>distortions</u>, <u>values</u>, <u>memories</u>, <u>assumptions</u>, <u>generalizations</u>, <u>hopes</u>, <u>dreams</u>... whatever it is that you have translated your sensory input history into. Any and all input goes through your filters, and your words are received through the listener's filters (as communication).

Your filters not only determine what you understand when others are talking to you, but they also formulate the manner with which you deliver a response. What are some of your favorite filters to use, and which filters drive you crazy when people use them in communication with you?

Know yourself.

Application: Landing Pages

Your website is an online retail storefront for your business. Landing pages (specific pages built for a specific deal or product) are the signs that draw customers in the door.

- <u>Step one</u>; figure out what you're offering.
- <u>Step two</u>; write a clear and concise call to action ("buy now"), and the

- <u>End result</u>; be sure that there is a simple way for you get people's contact information to follow up on (or simply sell the product right there).

Each time you use the tools, alter one of the pieces.

****
****

Once the information comes in and is filtered, then you get

3. Your version of the event: who, what, where, when, why, how of the experience.

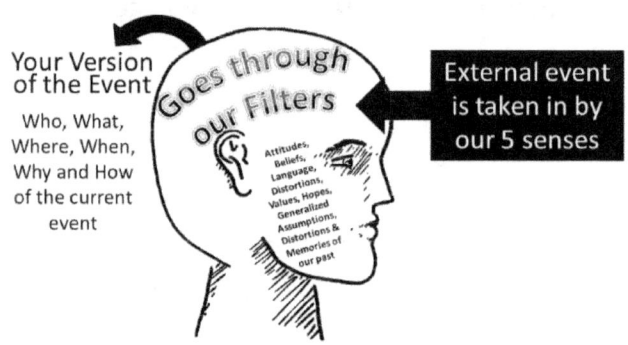

System of Human Communication:
The details and parameters of the event are sorted and filed into memory category (or categories)

Your Version of the Event
Who, What, Where, When, Why and How of the current event

Goes through our Filters

Attitudes, Beliefs, Language, Distortions, Values, Hopes, Generalized Assumptions, Distortions & Memories of our past

External event is taken in by our 5 senses

This is what we call a memory.

The mechanics of memory fit into our self-talk or internal process. It's never exactly what took place, but it's the version of what took place we have stored as a memory. Memories are most easily stored in our mental files *as the event is taking place*. Even though there are tools to adjust past memories—it's always harder to fix a false or destructive version of a memory after it's had time to take root in our emotions and mental video archives (the movies we create in our memory as we reply past events).

Some of your past experiences are painful, frightening, or sad because that is a reflection of what really happened. If your version of an event is completely inaccurate, it doesn't require that you have to experience the same feelings every time you remember it. Great communicators are able to free their memories from the state/filter/emotional experience they were having when the event occurred.

Sales Tip: Tell them what to think about

- Advanced sales professionals can tell their prospects what to think about—which determines what they will choose.

    o If your push is for something blue (during the presentation) you touch the items of clothing that are blue. This will urge them in the direction of something that is blue.

    o Use that color to your advantage. When you put together the proposal;

        • Use that color to communicate your priorities

        • You can also use words that rhyme with the color to coax them toward that color

        • If you want them to choose the green option you can ask, "where do you lean" "explain what you mean" or "this option is clean" … since our minds will naturally assume the one that rhymes is the one that "feels right"

    o These make you feel a little like you're not in control, unless you're the one in control

- **This works for all five senses, but (in the same manner that you don't like to be manipulated) don't be obvious or silly with these tools; or you will be the wizard that has the curtain pulled back and not even Toto will buy from you.**

* *

Once the information comes in and is filtered, then you impact

4. Emotional State that you're Currently Experiencing

This can determine what color, texture, scent, taste or tone we wrap the conversation into - before storing it as an event memory.

System of Human Communication:

External event, having passed our conscious and unconscious filters to make a version of the event combines with the state we are experiencing. These are typically stored together. The sensory input, filters and state at the time are packaged as an experience

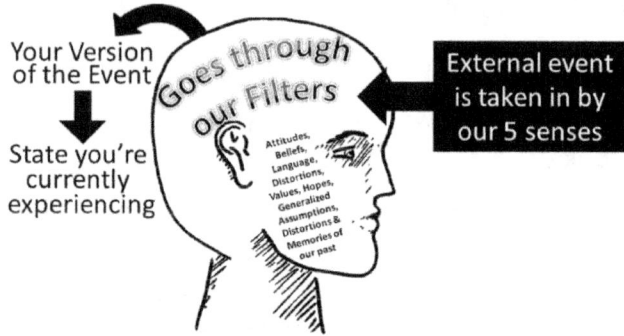

Your Version of the Event

Goes through our Filters

State you're currently experiencing

Attitudes, Beliefs, Language, Distortions, Values, Hopes, Generalized Assumptions, Distortions & Memories of our past

External event is taken in by our 5 senses

Your current mental state affects the version of your event in the present, how that event will pull up from your memory, how you're going to experience the recollection of the event down the road, and how you process what your next steps should be (based on the initial conversation).

Quite simply put, if you're in a bitchy mood, a common interaction can be translated into an offensive statement for no other (legitimate) reason than the mood that you were in yesterday was defensive. Often, the other person's statement was just an innocent observation while they were going about their day. People make statements that come across as something that is less than considerate, because they weren't considering me when they said it. Usually, other people aren't thinking of you at all when they speak; they're just living their life and you happened to be in their presence at the wrong time - it's nothing personal. They were busy living their life and had things on their mind... just like me... just like you.

If your current state affects your memory (and version of yesterday's events); then you made it a serious problem all on your own. Sorry, but you do have the ability to let it go.

Develop Leads into Clients

Information is everywhere if you're willing to look. There is a lot of web searching that can be done in exchange for an hour long face to face appointment. As a salesperson, overcome this loss of control through efficiency. Know what the modern sales and marketing tools are, and use them judiciously.

- **Ask, listen and then respond.**
- **Track follow up on every step, every time.**
- **Have scripts and use them always.**
- **Tell "your story" but focus on learning and knowing "their story" ("their story" is where the clues for why they will buy from you are hiding).**
- **Automate everything.**
- **Be your niche's expert.**

Be in the right place with the right mindset at the right time

****

If this was a counseling session, we could discuss experiential tactics that would help you understand why these behaviors are in place. This is not a counseling session; this is business. Stick to your purpose for the conversation.

- People don't know what your state is, but they assume your state by your behavior.

- Habitual behaviors that communicate a positive or negative state become recognized as a person's character.

- Many times, this realization only comes from those that know you best, but they're usually afraid to speak up because it's too real.

As you develop the internal skillset to intentionally communicate well, adjust your bad behavior to not be visible, **because it's bad for business**. Personal hang-ups make you less productive in the long run. Besides, you are only creating the wrong filters for the next encounter. Keep in mind; **It's not personal, it's business.**

Game: Emotional Trigger for Release

Recall past conversations that have affected the state that you experienced... even as long as weeks or months later.

Give yourself a _crazy phrase_ to use that resets your emotion and state when you find yourself in the wrong mindset for the situation at hand (say "Holy Guacamole" as an emotional trigger (if envy is what's being overcome) ... because envy and guacamole are both green. **Make it personal, effective and practiced to perfection.**

Provoke your own Reset.

For Instance: Forgiveness Frees the Forgiver

One of my favorite lessons is about how to handle those that offend and injure.

"If people are throwing rocks at you... we have a few options:

1. Some pick up the rocks and throw them back, because people who throw rocks either deserve it or need to know what it feels like when they're hit.

2. *Some pick up a rock for each person that threw it and put it in their pocket. Recording the name of the thrower on it so that they know who hurt them. At best they know the people to protect themselves from in the future, and at worst they can hold something against the throwers and know whom to get back when the opportunity presents itself.*

3. *Still others leave them on the ground. These are the ones that can look out for others and are light and free enough to move out of the way."*

Most of us throw them back or keep them in our pockets... and before we know it - we're the ones throwing the rocks (out of habit). It feels better to think that everyone owes us something... when all that I've done is weigh myself down.

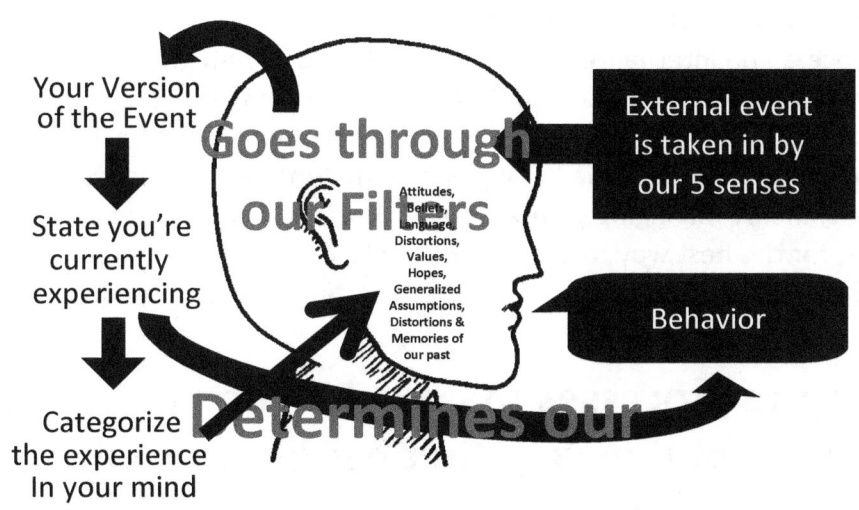

Process of Communication Wrap Up:

What are some of the general categories you use to classify people that are (and are not) what you're looking for? Use of the phrases, "pain in the ass" or "fun appointment", are filters that are being creating as you say them. Those filters wrap up memories **based on the state that you _were_ in when you stored a memory**. A past state can dramatically affect present experience.

- What filters are you currently creating through situations and relationships that you will experience this week?

- How would you rate your communication, and what is holding you back from being better?

If you don't answer that question now; you will likely never start. We receive about 2 million bits of information per second, but only process and internalize 128 of those bits. I love statistics like this. It means that we process 0.000064 percent of what we perceive. Put another way, we miss 99.9936% of what happens. That's a lot. Use the human mind you've been given; turn it into an excellence machine by managing your autopilot functions and keeping an eye out for the best way to use other people's auto-pilot. You can (through adjustments of our 'default' settings) become a super-communicator.

It's the processes that we function in (when we're not thinking) that has become who we are, but we can change that if we are intentional about our management of the pieces we've created.

A Couple of social interaction tips (for efficiency's sake)

Socially; **You get what you focus on.**

When I use negative language, I end up attracting people who are drawn to the negative (seems obvious). The issue with negative social interaction in business; whenever a client complains, you're supposed to respond with good customer service. If a client is a habitually negative talker, they will require much more time and energy than someone who sees and talks about the positive (typically).

In Person and Online Active Listening

Active Listening is... **when you reword everything that is being said to you into your own words while the other person is speaking.** The way that I become a better active listener, is through practice, one phrase at a time. A word from experience here; real active listening takes *a lot of energy*. In the same way that an athlete can work out for hours at a time but someone who doesn't work out will exhaust after a few minutes of warm-up... active listening is a taxing exercise that requires consistent application of new (commonly underused) muscles in focus. If you only try to do this once in a while—you will fail. If you make it a part of everyday life your strength and ability will grow. This is the best tool to really understand what someone is communicating when they are speaking.

Active Listening Steps:

1. **Pay attention**. Look only at your target, bring unconnected thoughts under control, and quit thinking about how you will respond (or anything that is not what they're communicating right now).

2. **Show you're following**: Nod or shake your head to encourage a yes or no and show you're tracking with what they're communicating. Make sure your face is saying what it's supposed to (pay attention to how your facial muscles feel when you use them for different

expressions). Some people frown or snarl instinctively when they listen—*don't' do this*. Give mini confirmations that you're tracking with them.

3. **Reiterate**: Give a second's pause when they're done to make sure they don't have anything else to add. In response to a lengthy statement, reply with, "What I hear you saying is...". Once you've given your metaphase, listen to make sure your interpretation is right.

Should I Keep **Personal and Business Separate**?

Our society champions our hero's abilities to keep their personal and business image in line; which is always (at some level) a lie. We also like to think we are held to a different standard than we hold our heroes. The standards in place today:

- Everything is connected

- You can lock accounts, but information has a consistent ability to become public

- You don't need to share everything (leave a little mystery to your life)

  o **This is a growing digital world that can breed fear and distrust in many.** There are tools that invade privacy available everywhere. The ability to find (and even use) information, doesn't mean you have to share that you have it. Not all knowledge needs to be public.

I have found that the online persona we present... resembles public speaking.

*When speaking; I prepare and plan how each part will seamlessly fit together to communicate a solid concept in a cleaver manner that will provoke gratitude in my listeners. **What happens: I open my mouth (or start to type) and the truth comes out.** Just try to be the best possible version of yourself; in both your personal and business online presence (and when you're giving a speech).*

5. Analyze and Adjust moment by moment (Fish in Net)

Analysis and Review of fishing for business is an internal game. The most common obstruction to success is; having a past assumption (or an "anchor") in your mindset that is pulling you in a direction other than what your business plan outlines. **It's all about figuring out what is producing results and why.**

Be Flexible enough to see past yourself

Many times choosing to be flexible requires severing parts of your physical makeup that are actively rewarding you for maintaining connection. Connections in our brain weigh down our functioning like anchors. Our behavior is based on the "anchors" we have created throughout our lives (starting in the womb). You made connections while reading this. "Anchors" are internal responses to an internal or an external experience.

Whether we have an understanding as to why an anchor is in place or not, there is always a point of legitimacy (or it would not have been created). **Problem anchors are exposed when a response is disproportionate to the situation**, or when the manner with which you engage is not in line with intent.

Recognizing what these anchors are and when they are triggered is the goal.

It is one thing to know what behavioral anchors are in you; but it is absolutely vital to recognize the triggers that lead up to activating the anchors (so that you can be flexible *in your behavior* when others' anchors drag you in an unexpected direction). If you can see a hard turn coming; you can prepare yourself to be able to react in an intentional fashion (though it won't feel natural), rather than purely on instinct and emotion. **Anchors are real and carry enormous power, but they are not outside your control.** Not all anchors that are disproportionate or that are inappropriate are negative.

Some anchors are beneficial. With any anchor, it's wise to consider:

- Uniqueness of your stimulus that triggers it
- Intensity of your response to the situation
- Purity of your end purpose
- Timing of when it is (and is not) appropriate
- Context for when you want this to be a part of your behavior

Hunting: identify target, plan attack, pursue, eat (when fishing becomes 1 on 1)

1. What are you currently doing?
2. Identify Your Target & Action
3. Campaign Design
4. Schedule Activity
5. Negotiation Preparation
6. Analyze and Adjust (weekly-monthly)

1. What are you currently doing?

Assess your Client Base (for Target Identification):

Select which client type to focus on. Previous or current paying clients who have required the <u>least amount of time</u>, but made the <u>most money</u> create a model for your business that is the most sustainable.

Assess your Existing Pipeline (definition in "Campaign Design"):

I over-assume what I can get done in one year, and under estimate what I can get done in five years. Today, a customer is in control of the first third to two-thirds of the sales pipeline. Long-term success is hinged on an accurate ratio of completed activity (stuffing the pipe of a pipeline) - to the income generated (catching the mud out the other side). This ratio is one of the primary benefits of web analytics. If you know the number of website visitors necessary to produce a lead; you can adjust activity to increase the visitors required to match income needs.

<u>THE QUESTIONS TO ASK (below: super-simple pipeline outline (worksheet follows):</u>

- How many calls, emails, social media connections, or conversations do I need to initiate **before I get a lead**?

- How many **leads for one 1st appointment**?

- How many **1st appointments before one proposal**?

- How many **proposals for a sale**?

Assess and Control Yourself (as a sales person):

In sales (like acting), it doesn't matter what you are actually feeling… you have a role to play and your priority and emotional state are a part of the description within the role you're playing.

Define: What are States and Emotions? A State is a combination of the physical and mental influences that encompass the 'to be' verb; i.e. "I am" or "She is". Emotions are what we attach to the chemicals that run through our body as a response (or result of) how circumstances make us feel (our state).

The mind and will fight with the body for your actions. At times, it is a knock down drag out, in your face fight, and at other times it is a sly and underhanded manipulation that you don't catch—until it's too late.

**Story:** _There once was a man who raised racing dogs. He had two of the fastest that the county dog track had ever seen. After a year of these two taking first and second every race (and the clerk that takes bets recognizing that he chose the right dog every time) ... the clerk inquired how he could know which dog would win._ **_The dog owner said, "Oh, it's simple._** _Whichever dog I feed—he's the one that wins."_

We are as strong as the part of ourselves we feed. If we satisfy each and every emotional urge, we shouldn't be shocked when they get the best of us.

Quota Layout
Assess your current quota system:

The word "Quota" has a history based on sales managers hounding staff to do the mundane tasks that the managers receive bonuses from. Quotas; however, are a way to complete the tasks that push mud in the front of the pipeline; in order to get a consistent flow of income out the back of the pipeline.

Questions when creating a quota (combined with Step 1):

- What is your **average income on a sale**?
- How much do you **need to make on a monthly basis**?

- How many average **sales needed**, in order to create your **monthly income** necessary to cover your annual lifestyle?
- Break it down into weekly quotas so you know, "This week, I need to make five in-person visits," or, "This week I need to send 35 emails or 15 direct messages on social network in order to make the income that my lifestyle demands. "

Create a quota. **Stuff the mud in the front and get paid.**

Sales Team Quota breakdown numbers—Long pipeline:
Every pipeline point of contact needs to be included

7 RATIO NUMBERS FROM PIPELINE TO QUOTA:
(A) Need: __3____ closing appointments to get a sale
(B) Need: __6____ qualifying appointment to get a closing appointment
(C) Need: __3____ introductions to get a qualifying appointment
(D) Need: __2___ leads to get an introduction appointment
(E) We typically make $2,500__ per sale
(F) Desired monthly income per sales rep: $7,500
(G) Number of sales reps for which leads are provided: __18__

LEADS NEEDED PER REP. CALCULATIONS:
- (A): _3_ x (B) __6__ = **(H) Qualifying appointments per mo.: __18__**
- (H): __18__ x (C) __3__ = **(I) Introductions per mo.: __54__**
- (I): _54__ x (D): _2_ = **(J) Number of leads to get a sale: _108_**
- (F): ___$7,500___ / (E): ___$2,500__ = **(K) Sales quota/mo: __3___**
- (J): ____108____ x (K): __3_ = **(L) Leads needed per month: __324_**

TEAM LEADS CALCULATION (WEEKLY):
- (G): _18__ x (L): ___324_ = **(M) Team leads per month: __5,832__**
- (M): _5,832_ / 4.33 (weeks/mo in 13 wk quarter) = **_1,347/wk.**

- *Question is*: does your marketing provide the leads you are needing to hit your outcomes/quotas?
- *If no, there's two options*: Increase your leads, or decrease the pipeline ratios of your sales team.

Sample Pipeline Assessments (from scripts section)

ABC Offices Current Pipeline:
1. Receive phone call lead looking for new office space
2. Call back within two days & ask to meet or leave message
3. When they call back ask if they want to come by office
4. Once they come by the office, show them around
5. Send them home with brochure and set follow up
6. Call back in a week & ask if they are interested
7. Keep on mailing list if "no" response
8. Set closing appointment
9. Show offices and present paperwork
10. If no sale, set for follow up in a month
11. Follow up in 6 months to see if they're ready to move yet

XZY Barbers Current Pipeline:
1. Run ads in men's magazines and online directories
2. When they call, record the name, phone and time they want to have an appointment
3. Give them a business card with their barber's name and book next appointment before leaving
4. Ask for Referral we could send a care package to
5. Offer discount if they give a review before the next service

6. Repeat when they call again for another shave or haircut

John Doe Current Pipeline:
1. Get contact information for a lead from an event or referral
2. Call or email the lead to set meeting in coffee shop
3. Have an introductory meeting to get to know each other
4. Do research on what product fits the lead
5. Call or email within 1 week to pitch the product/service
6. If they're responsive, set a proposal appointment
7. Prepare for the proposal meeting by printing materials and paperwork for lead (to leave with them)
8. Call 24 hours in advance to confirm the appointment
9. Proposal Meeting at quieter location, preferably with a computer or projector available (conference room/office)
10. Ask for the sale after giving the proposal or set a next step
11. Call 24 hours in advance to confirm the appointment
12. Call in 1 week if no response to set closing appointment
13. Call 24 hours in advance to confirm the appointment
14. Print paperwork for closing appointment
15. Build rapport; ask if they have questions, and close
    a. If no, thank them for their time and set follow up in 6 mo.'s
16. Call in 24 hours to thank them & gauge why not interested
17. Place on mailing list

Assess States and Emotions

What state-of-mind are you in?

- On Monday Mornings?
  _____

- When you have a face to face meeting with a new prospect:
  _____

- On Friday Afternoon?
  _____

What is my current state?

Physically:

_____

Mentally:

_____

Behavior arises out of your state
- Some states make behavior difficult to do anything productive
- Some states make the most daunting tasks seem effortless & fluid
- What are some of the factors that go into making your state one that will make your behavior as productive and fluid as possible?

_____

How do we create our states?
- Mentally Define our States as something we are experiencing (not what's happening to us).

  _____Breathing (experience)_____

  _Muscle Tension & Posture (trigger)_____

Choosing your state is not "looking on the bright side", but rather seeing our state as 'action signals' that are directing us to awareness for what our body and mind are experiencing (and which require our attention).

Recognizing the states of others: Look around the room and tell what states each person is in currently.

Provoking an optimal state in others takes one of two paths:
1. Thinking yourself into a new state (imagine a time when...)
2. Acting yourself into a new state (get up & move, vary breathing by changing topic)

Since you can't always know the state you're in... have set replies for the most common interactions.

Cut or Reinforce your Personality Anchors

Behavioral Flexibility:
We create connections in our brain "Anchors" that tie an internal response with an (internal or external) experience. These almost always have a point of legitimacy, or they would not have been created.

When the response seems disproportionate to the situation - there is usually an Anchor involved

- What do you respond to (that others see as disproportioned)?

    o Bad Feelings:

    _____

    o Good Feelings:

    _____

Other People: when you notice someone has a response that doesn't seem reasonable; recognize that they are having an anchor drag, and your response is to be flexible in your behavior... **it's not all about you**, even though you're the one in control **(if you're willing to be flexible)**.

Recognize the following anchor signals (when you're setting an anchor): Uniqueness of Stimulus, Intensity, Purity, Timing, Context (they only work in the context they are created).

Be Sensitive to your Surroundings

"The most important thing in communication is to hear what is not being said." (quote by Peter Druker)

Observation: is what you notice with your five senses
Interpretation: is when you create a conclusion about what that information means/intent behind the action
- We all have skills set up to calibrate how these function together, we just aren't conscious of them

What to pay attention to in Developing your Calibration Skills
- **Your Posture**: What are your default positions when you are excited, alert, relaxed, etc.

- **Physical Tells**: Purposeless movements... gestures, jiggles & taps of appendages, location and depth of breath, pitch, tempo, rhythm and volume of voice (record yourself if you need to)

View of others
Behind every behavior is positive intention (somewhere)
- People make the best choices available to them
    - At that moment
    - With their history
    - Knowing what they know
    - In their belief structure
    - With the resources at their disposal
    - Viewed from their frame of reference
        - People make the best choices available to them

Give your energy and effort to uncovering the positive motivation that is the springboard for other's behavior; respond to that.

Control States & Emotions

Don't sabotage your own success

States and emotions are the most visible unquantifiable pieces of self. What state are you in? What emotion are you experiencing? How much of each? In order to control states and emotions, first we must recognize how different circumstances provoke and soothe you. We like to live in denial because our culture considers emotion during business to be weak. That could not be farther from the truth. These are real chemical influences that gauge, alter, and determine our decisions.

It is difficult to assess emotions and states that are not current. If we are in the midst of an experience, it is a reflex to forget our intent and succumb to the state brought on by the emotional pull of the moment, that (in comparison) is weak.

At times the physical stimulation and the mental decisions we have made for 'future actions' stand in conflict with each other. Both have influence over each other, but one will always win out.

Since behavior arises out of your state, identify the states that make a desired behavior difficult. Other states can make the most daunting tasks seem effortless. Know yourself.

Define: Addiction to Emotions?

- **Emotions aren't good or bad:** They are simply pieces of who we are. Emotion chemicals (like all stimuli) naturally carry the ability to allow addiction. Heroin uses the same cell receptors that emotions use.

- **The more we infuse our bodies with the chemicals** for a certain emotion, **the more our body will create an appetite for that chemical**. The "that's enough" counter balance chemicals will be reduced, and the receptors for the emotion we are embracing will increase.

- **The incredible truth is;** the more we experience an emotion (no matter how harmful), the more we begin to feel like an expert in that state (and refuse to listen to anyone else), because they don't have the experience that we do... which is correct. If they had our experience, they would not have the insight to recognize our addiction. They would be fellow addicts or co-dependent.

How do we create our state?

1. States are a map to our future behavior.

A map can tell you where you are going, but it can only be written in review of where you have been. Tracking the <u>internal and external signals</u> that predict what our body and mind are experiencing... is the first step to gaining control over our states and emotions:

- How are you breathing?
- What is your posture?
- Where is your muscle tension?
- What were the physical signs and symptoms that lead up to an event or experience I'd like to replicate (or avoid) in the future?

Nothing will happen without our purposeful attention. Just like any experiment, adjusting our mental state requires mapping and designing the factors. Self-awareness is difficult, but worthwhile.

2. It's not all about you.

It would be truly difficult to have to personally experience everything before we could learn anything. Recognizing the states and emotions of others is not only important to predict *their* behavior, but it is the quickest and easiest path to gain understanding without the requirement of experience. Look outside yourself.

3. Assessing is not Judging.

There is a marked difference between paying attention to the people around you for the sake of understanding... and allowing the assessment to inform the state you attribute to others.

At the point that an observation ends with, "because they...", the shift from understanding to judging has taken place.

- Is your typical response to others a question or a statement?

- Are you intrigued or annoyed at people who are not like you?

Game: Guess their State

- What do you pay attention to when tracking the people around you?

- What can you guess about their state?

- Have you incorrectly assumed other's states in the past?

- What are your common states that you assume for others? (assume right and assume wrong)

    This is an activity that requires practice. Guess what state they're in and pay attention to their behavior. See if your assumption is correct by interacting with them.

Exercises to develop Behavioral Muscles:

If it takes place inside your mind:

- It affects you.

- The chemical response we categorize as emotions are real internal receptor connections in our bodies.

- It is potentially within your control.

Ways to provoke a preferred state (one of two paths)

1. **Thinking yourself into a new state.**

    If I want to overcome my desire to avoid an activity (like Cold Calling), I need to adjust how I tell myself the memory. Go through the memory, and **alter** the most **powerful emotional source in the memory.** They say in depression there's a hushed voice in your head; it's so quiet and soothing that it draws you into its grasp.

    - *Change the whisper into a clown with a high-pitched squeaking. Whatever voice you hear, alter that voice. Adjust it so that it will lose its power. Adjust how you see it, what it is currently, how it has control. Make it change with how you see, hear, and feel the video as it plays.*

    Sales Tip: Reset Yourself: At times things happen that cause one or both parties to disengage (or become defensive). Sometimes circumstance will cause an influential level of like or dislike towards each other. When you find yourself in the wrong state in sales:

    - **RESET MATRA, "I'm here to do a job, so it doesn't matter how I think about them, feel about them, or whether I want to engage them. I will do my job well. "**

    - **Options for a reset: There have been a number of sales appointments that I have said, *"I need to run out to the car/bathroom really quick. Do you mind if I do that?"***

        1. Stepping out of the room by running to the car or using the restroom allows me to change my breathing patterns and refocus my purpose... I can *act myself into a new state.*

2. At times it's not possible. Take a 3 breath :15
   second break to *think myself free*. Pretend to
   search an answer on your phone or give them
   permission to answer a call.

2. Acting yourself into the new state.

On either of these two paths; there are a number of exercises
that can be used to develop the muscles that influence our
behavioral state. Keep in mind; your practicing the exercise
doesn't mean that you are exercising. If you do three pushups
ever hour for a day, it doesn't mean that you are going to
experience the same results as someone who does 50
pushups every morning.

These four behavioral muscles overviewed below are only a
glimpse of what's available. There are as many options for
exercise as there are ways to get your heart rate up when
working out our physical bodies. Just get moving in the right
direction.

Behavioral Muscles; action paths to build virtue:

Behavioral Muscle: **Thankfulness**
- BENEFIT: Like most muscles, being thankful has as much (if not
  more) benefit for the one exercising the muscle as it does for those
  who surround, but both are rewarded.
- EXERCISE: Request vs Complaint: Spend an hour or two in a public
  place, and for each complaint you hear, reword it in your mind into
  a request. Progress may be tracked by recording the translations in
  a journal or notepad. What are they really asking for? Who is
  capable of fulfilling this request? Describe how the request would
  look, if fulfilled. **Any complaint translated into a request allows
  completion.** The complaint is moved to a position in which we can
  express gratitude if and when that desire is fulfilled.
- WARNING: Resist justification. All complaints have a basis. All lack of
  gratitude is based on something we think we deserve. Our history
  and experience determine the amount of privilege and entitlement

we deem "expected", and anything on top of that we naturally feel thankfulness. Move that bar.

Behavioral Muscle: **Patience**
- BENEFIT: One of the biggest detriments to sales success is pressing when you should pause. Patience is one of the most under-valued characteristics in our society founded on instant gratification. Lack of this value is why we don't understand that patience is exactly why we typically get in our own way.
- EXERCISE: This is one of the disciplines that **requires an absence of action**.
- WARNING: Hesitation is a great supplement to fear, but hesitation has nothing to do with real patience. This behavioral muscle is (rather) *not acting when our emotions are pushing us to pull the trigger*, and not an excuse to make inaction appear righteous... to protect the coward.

Behavioral Muscle: **Humility**
- BENEFIT: We, as humans, have a tendency to process everyone and everything through a selfish lens. Most (except for the self-delusional and vain) respect someone who is humble (because all great people know one thing... that they don't know everything).
- SAMPLE EXERCISE: Pick a day of the week that you allow everyone with a desire to get in front of you in a line—to do so. Be careful to not harm the well-being of those behind you (by never taking a turn), but with so many pushing to be first—be the one that is patient... allowing others to get in front of you. Humility is only grown through service (and unrecognized service at that).
- WARNING: Do not allow yourself to require a specific response or "thank you" from those you allow to be first. If you exercise only when others recognize you—you will lose all benefit the exercise.

Behavioral Muscle: **Self Control**
- BENEFIT: The ability to have every sensation satisfied with almost no physical exertion of energy has caused our natural hierarchy of needs to be interrupted by the confusion of need vs. want, what I deserve and obvious excess, as well as pain and lack of fulfilled demand. Non-stop input doesn't allow us to sort and file knowledge to understanding or wisdom.

- EXERCISE: Fasting from input. Fasting is the voluntary denial of an appetite for the sake of personal control and growth (in the areas you can't see). Typically fasting involves refraining from eating food for a matter of days, but the most beneficial fast I've experienced is called a "word fast". I like to talk, so reserving one day to listen without allowing myself to add anything to a conversation... exposed me to how useless most small talk is, how oblivious most of us are to what we say, and (most vitally) that the world runs just fine without my words being added.
- WARNING: Almost every member of the developed world lives a more extravagant and posh life than many aristocrats throughout history. We don't plant, harvest, draw water, catch or prepare food. We cook food that was prepared and has been packaged for us - based on servicing size. We are not subject to the seasons of the year, time of day, or limitations of distance. Your physical body will scream that you are going against your best interests (as well as the laws of this physical realm) when you deny impulses and cut off input. This is almost always an appetite throwing a fit that it's not being fed. Our chemical addiction to demand fulfillment carries a serious set of withdrawals and symptoms.

Safeguard yourself from yourself:

Since you can't always predict the state you're going to be in after someone cuts you off in traffic, have set replies for the most common circumstance. Comedians use the same joke night after night after night, and I can guarantee that after the 35th time they've said it, it's usually not as funny (to them). However, it is usually the first time their audience has heard it, so it's their job to pretend they're telling it brand new.

Write out a couple <u>Behavioral Muscle</u>, <u>Benefit</u>, <u>Exercise</u>, and <u>Warning</u> for each Behavioral Muscle you'd like to work out until it becomes muscles of character.

<u>Behavioral Muscle I want to work on:</u> _____

- <u>BENEFIT</u>:

\
\
_____

_____

_____

- <u>EXERCISE</u>:

\
\
_____

_____

_____

- <u>WARNING</u>:

\
\
_____

_____

_____

2. Identify Your Target & Action

Lead List/Categorization

- It is necessary to have a consistent categorization system and use it on every lead.
- If you don't have the right categorization, you may end up calling a cold prospect instead of a warm or hot one... just because you didn't remember how they were categorized and you only had 10 minutes to make 3 calls before your next appointment.

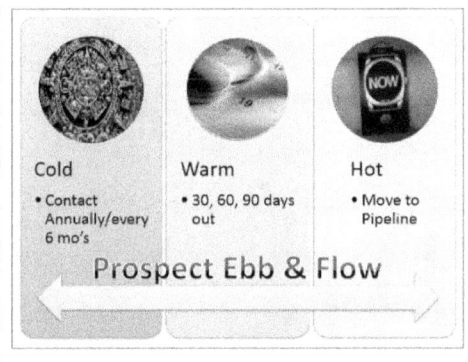

List a few prospects that you think fit into these categories:

- Cold: _____

_____ _____
_____ _____
_____ _____

- Warm: _____

_____ _____
_____ _____
_____ _____

- Hot: _____

_____ _____

As with most of the other pieces of this pipeline set up:
- Make it work for you
- Use the categorizations you currently use (you built it on purpose)
- No matter what you call them, clarify in your system the type of lead it is so you can make sure you give the limited time you have to the hottest prospects you have in your system.

How does a client talk (Conversational Perspectives)?

Conversational Perspectives

These perspectives are the dance that create the perceptions each party brings to the table, developing into rapport—or loss. Be able to communicate any given circumstance from each of these three perspectives (upon request). This will increase your ability to translate what the other person is thinking and communicating.

First person: When you see things from your own point of view.

We all live and communicate from this point of view. We can only imagine and articulate another view or perspective by guessing. This *IS* where you are coming from. This perspective can be typically characterized by:

- The words "I" and "Me"
- Telling stories about yourself
- "Explaining your own opinion" and "typical internal dialogue" are examples of first person
- When you're aware of the feelings in your own body, it's first person

Don't get stuck thinking it's always bad to function in the first person.

- **The upside**: this perspective is assertive to express your own point of view, because often you do know more than the person sitting across from you. *You should if you're in sales.*

- **The downside**: this perspective is very seductive (to *live* in first person), and close your eyes to the outside world... it's just a waste of a life.

- **The truth is**: everyone knows that this is a perspective from which we all approach every negotiation (and almost every conversation). We live in first person. You're a part of the meeting for a reason. Trick is to not get stuck being focused on this perspective so long that you start to believe that any meeting or group is actually all about you (or that the other person should be understanding enough to see the conversation from your view). **That would be called narcissistic.**

- ***The goal is***: *To get outside of isolation and see things from another person's point of view.*

Second Person: When you see things from the other person's point of view.

*This perspective can be dangerous in its confusion, because it's a deflected 1st person perspective. If you are able to understand that you are viewing their perspective (**through your life, map and view**)—there is a possibility to actually use the Second person perspective (even though you aren't seeing anything from another's actual perspective - only your viewpoint pretending to be from theirs). The tactics on 'mirroring' (in the negotiation section that follows) are tools that help to draw other's trust while in second person.*

This is characterized by:

- The words "You" or "in her shoes"
- Asking questions, and listening to the answers

- Mirroring the person, you're in a conversation with for the purpose of comprehending perspective

*My wife teases me that she can tell the ethnicity, age range and gender of whoever I'm on the phone with. It's not because I falsely pretend I'm them (or that I pick up their accent leading them to believe I'm Irish when speaking with somebody who's Irish) ... **but, I can mirror them in pacing the response with which I listen and engage.** Besides, I can't do accents... every accent I do sounds like a mix between bad Chinese and Scottish accents— but I can engage a conversation I'm in from the second person perspective.*

- **The upside:** The longer you engage this perspective the more you learn the "why" of their decisions, and allow yourself to connect and actually communicate.

- **The downside:** If you only engage in this perspective you will be dismissed as a fake because everyone knows you're actually there in first person (everyone is). You have a selfish perspective for being in the business negotiation... even if you're representing a philanthropic purpose... and trying to help them... you're doing it for your own purposes.

- **Truth is:** Even when you're engaging from the second person you're still engaging as yourself. You're trying to put yourself in the other person's position, but you'll never do it exactly. You don't know their map of the world—so you're guessing.

- ***The goal is:*** *When you're in second person, become completely aware of the five senses that the other person is experiencing. Understand their experience, not just their words.*

Third Person: When you see things from the detached observer viewpoint.

This is *very* powerful in negotiation (especially when the conversation is stuck). This perspective is typically characterized by:

- Words like "from a 30,000-foot view I see" or "What I hear us saying is"
- Spoken as a witness of what's happening
- Listening to how one person's comments are translated by the another

Third person detachment allows you to analyze a situation with no regard for how it affects either party.

- **The upside:** When conflict or emotion arise (viewing the room in a "hover mode"), a 30,000-foot view exposes selfless resolve and clarity.

- **The downside:** If you get caught in this viewpoint for more than a quick realization you'll be categorized as impersonal, distant, and disinterested. Also, in the social media comments world, people (usually) aren't looking for a resolution, just a place to express whatever is in their head... and a "can't we all just get along" response is worse than no response, because it doesn't consider the setting's communication standards and... that's annoying.

- **The truth is:** If you are in a negotiation, and two other people are the main voices in the discussion; this offers you the ability to listen, hear and translate each of them, and possibly meta-phrase where they're both coming from to create a baseline from which the negotiation can grow. This is an opportunity to establish yourself as someone who should be a part of the negotiation (when you've been cut out).

- ***The goal is:*** *Either give a summary and create a checkpoint for negotiation, or offer insight when a juggernaut has been able to sabotage progress.*

Test your Scripts: (painful mastery task)

This exercise was briefly covered before, but beneficial enough to add here as well.

The two pieces to this step are:

  1) Record yourself

  2) Go back and type out or transcribe what you have spoken (word for word)

Take each of the steps that you've included in Scripts, and record yourself speaking your part for each of them - from each of these conversational perspectives.

- **Record your speaking**

- **Transcribe your speaking to text**

  There is a power that comes from having to transcribe what you say. When you transcribe the recording of your presentation—be certain to type out each "um", "ah", heavy breath, and spit or slurp.

Point is: If it's painful for you to listen to and transcribe, how much more painful is it going to be for everyone to listen to you do the exact same thing. We all have "idiot-syncrocies" that show up in how we come across to others. Usually, they're just too polite to tell you that you make funny noises and that you spit (video would catch the later error).

DON'T SKIP THE "TEST THE SCRIPTS" STEP.

This may be the most painful, but it's one of the most valuable.

3. Campaign Design

<u>What is a Pipeline & Why does it Matter?</u>

Every sales process is like a pipeline... Some are long and skinny (take a long time to close, and have a small number of contacts pass through the pipe), and some are short and fat (require a lot of new leads, but have a short turn around between connection and sale). Each service and product has a pipeline that is unique. A sales person begins prospecting by stuffing mud (activity) in one end of that pipe, and eventually it starts coming out the other side. A pipeline is not adjustable; it is solid and calculable. It doesn't change. Once you've designed your pipeline; you know... if the activity is stuffed in the front side, eventually money will start coming out the other.

Many times, as sales people see the mud exiting the pipe (make sales and bring in money), they quit stuffing the front - because they think they have completed all the hard work they need to do. The pipe dries up, mud quits being pushed out, and you don't understand why your system quit working. So you start going back to the beginning and doing the hard work, but there's a long dry spell before anything comes out. **The trick to sales is to keeping pushing mud (sales activity) in one side while it flows out the other side (sales income).** When sales activity stops, your pipeline dries up and you get hungry.

<u>Rule of Thumb: 1 in 60</u>

This rule states that for every 1 degree off heading, a ship will be 1 mile off course for every 60 miles it travels, 2 miles off at 120, 4 at 240, etc.

<u>Example of the 1 in 60 rule (as it pertains to sailing to Hawaii):</u>

If you're sailing from L.A. to Hawaii (4105km/2551 mi), and you get 2 degrees off track from the onset of the trip (which is 1/3 of 1 minute on a clock), you would be over 100km off course once you traveled the correct distance... which is problematic because after some cool math (involving a cosine value that is approximately 0.0454 degrees) ... you will miss your target by over 60 miles.

<u>Computer Work: Have scripts for email automation:</u> We all have times that our behavioral state is not in line with the person we want to be. There are a number of situations that controlling your response is as simple as writing a script, and using it.

- **<u>Where to save pre-written email templates</u>: If your inbox has "templates" or "Canned Responses" - create one. If it doesn't, create a document as "email scripts" that are titled by when you use it, and includes the text of the email correspondence. Be willing to include a [PLACEHOLDER] for custom words or phrases that will be edited each time that email template is used.**

Go through the most common responses you give and write them down. As a sales person you're an actor, but not all of your lines require that you deliver them in person. Make your scripts as enjoyable as possible and allow your state to be controlled by what you have predetermined when you're in a good mood - rather than speaking as a victim of circumstance.

Simplify your steps to stay out of your own way

4. Schedule Activity

Expectations; We over assume what we can get done in one year, and under estimate what we can get done in five years.

<u>Define: Buying Cycle, Pipeline, and Pitch</u> (repeated for convenience)

- <u>Pitch or Ask</u>: Question that (when answered) closes the negotiation.

- <u>Buying Cycle</u>: The cycle of; marketing to sale to referral (that almost all business communication follows).

  - This is the normal cycle of business. Recognize; the client only focuses on this buying cycle once in a while (so continual hand holding is likely needed and productive).

- <u>Pipeline</u>: The process of tracking one company or individual through the buying cycle; ensuring that no one is lost or allowed to continue too far.

<u>Make **Preparation, Next Step** and **Reminder** for each Pipeline Segment:</u>

Every point of contact in the pipeline has associated **preparation**, **next step** and **reminder** tasks. Even if the next step in the pipeline is a quick email, there is a: **preparation**; a mental review of the last conversation (which on a quick email is written as a personal comment in the email), **next step**; instructions for the task you will complete (also in the quick email for clear expectations) when the next **reminder** shows up in your CRM on the scheduled day/time... if you enter it in your CRM.

A Reschedule Process ensures that you know what to do if your next step is cancelled vs. a no show. It is also a vital piece of a pipeline to know which steps (in the pipeline) you run into a, "I'm not going to do business with them" or Kill-the-Deal checkpoint.

A sales mentor I had when I first started selling used the phrase

"If it's a loser, lose early."

Sales Tip: Design Your Day

Proper assessment of who you are and the conversations you will (likely) have, can allow you to arrange the plain, mundane tasks that you are required to do (and are capable of auto-pilot completion) **… to be scheduled during the time of day that you are not most productive.** If you hate data entry, do it after lunch when you're not overly excited about working (and need something to keep you moving forward). It keeps you awake & busy.

> *Story: I personally am not best in the morning. I don't easily get back into my body once I've been sleeping, and that has (in the past) created a bad state of mind. I avoid disciplining my daughters in the mornings due to my tendency to overreact (not hear correctly) … In some way engage with more passion and energy than is right.*

In the same way, use the times of day you're most productive for the tasks that require the most focus (and the best parts of you).

Every job has parts that you love and… don't love. Arrange them so you are most productive and enjoy the maximum portion. Design your day for happiness in success.

Pipeline Reschedule guide

It takes as much time to click "delete" as it does to click the date for call back. A lead is never deleted, unless the lead requests it, Even if you have them on a "call once a year" reminder system... contact once a year It is easiest if you set up your database follow ups - to fit the pipeline structure you set up. If the call back schedule in your CRM is based on the categories listed below, you will only have to change the status of the lead, next step, and call back date to be able to keep track of every client you want to keep in the pipeline. I also suggest a date stamped note for each step.

This is only a sample from which you can have a framework.

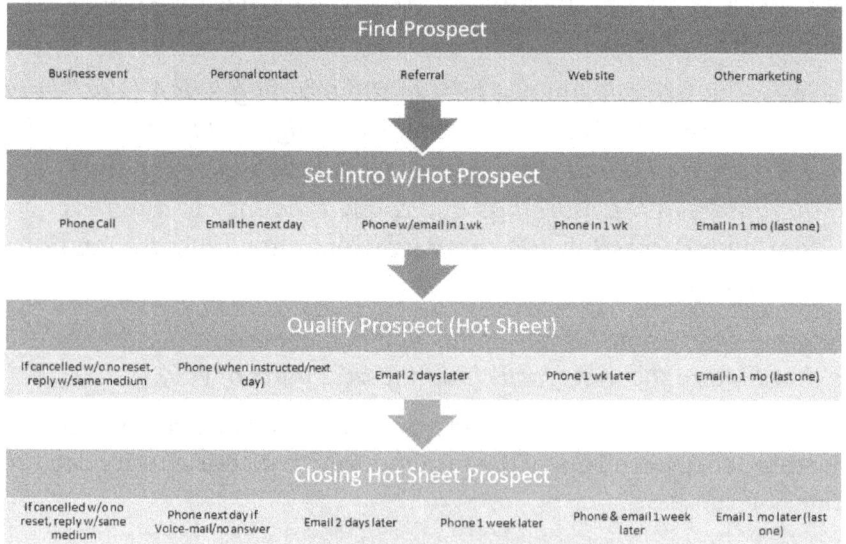

Pipeline Steps

In any pipeline, there are times you need to assess whether you want this prospect to be a client
- If they are high maintenance before they sign up with you, what do you think they are going to be after?
- The stars in this pipeline represent the times that you should assess whether you want them to be a client or not
  - If not, refer them to someone else
  - Let them know you don't think there's a fit for you to do business OR
  - Price it high enough that you can outsource the work and still make it worth your while

This pipeline should be coupled with a CRM that tracks each lead that is found

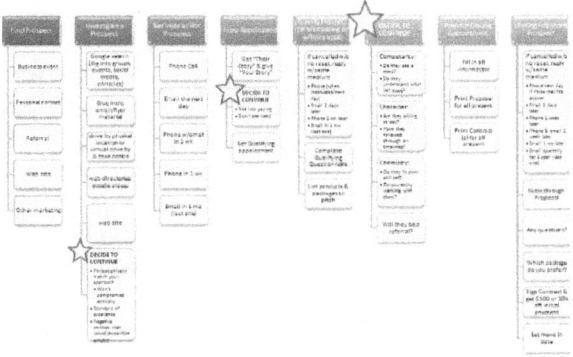

Pipeline Design Template ***

Pipeline Step: _____

This step is a success for me when: _____

They will benefit from this appointment when: _____

Before the next appointment:

- I am committing that I will: _____

- I am asking them to: _____

If they cancel or don't show, my follow up:

Scripts & Materials to Write: _____

Immediate response: _____

After ___ days, I'll _____ (action)

Who else needs to be involved: _____

After ___ days, I'll _____
My confirmation tasks: _____

After ___ days, I'll _____
Days I need to Prep: _____

Pipeline Reponses

Define your Buying Cycle

Business includes finesse and style and intentionality... that must be developed. This requires discipline and commitment to prepare the pieces with attention and patience (to do what you need to do) each day. *With that warning label attached; **this is a skill and not a talent... so it can be modeled and learned with effort.***

A vendor walks through buying cycle conversations many times a month, typically. The buyer (on the other hand) is constantly in an uncomfortable and abnormal state of transition and flux. To make it worse; the buyer is often the only one who is going to live with the ramification of the decision (whereas the vendor is going to be making money on the next deal). Many times the buyer has never done this before; and they are moving from one unfamiliar step to another (as sales impatience increases)—toward or away from the exchange of money. A clear understanding and empathy of the buyer's process will allow you to push, pause and ask the right questions (at the right times).

Buying cycle steps:

Write the responses you'll use here and type them out in your mail program or scripts documents. Use your phrases of speech and slang (because that's how you talk).

1. **No interest:** Many people will tell you this. It is impossible to determine (absolutely) when a person is ready to buy—that is why we market. This is also why we aim at <u>T</u>op <u>Of</u> the <u>M</u>ind <u>A</u>wareness <u>T</u>hrough <u>O</u>thers (T.O.M.A.T.O.).

- Preparation (communicate regret):

  _____

- Next Step (communicate expectation):

  _____

- Reminder (set reminder w/note):

  _____

2. **The buyer identifies a need**: *(This is a temporary state)* The buyer might identify their need through something they saw, a conversation they had, or an email they received. It could have been provoked by someone they know who experienced the resolution of whatever pain this purchase is remedying... but at some point the buyer identifies their need *(and this is temporary)*.

   - Preparation (reword the need with your product names):

     _____

   - Next Step (if I put together... you agree that you will...):

     _____

   - Reminder (set reminder w/note):

     _____

- **I want to Research the Options.** Whether they are searching or not, this is often the response soon after identifying the need—it appears to be continuous. Recognition of the need opens the buyer's senses, so that they start through their information gathering process.

   - Preparation (list referral source and top 3 options):

     _____

   - Next Step (list primary of research categories):

     _____

   - Reminder (set reminder w/note):

     _____

- **Buyer is questioning the price**. Includes (but is not limited to) time, money, attention, and focus. There is more to a buying decision than cost vs. price. Cost is obviously what sales people pay the most attention to since paychecks are tied to it. Cash to pay for a need to be resolved is only one of the resources that is calculating when deciding whether to say yes or no.
    - Preparation (Unique Value Proposition):
      _____
    - Next Step (ask):
      _____
    - Reminder (set reminder w/note):
      _____

- **Buyer Selects the Resolution, but not your product.** The buyer will typically think they've done all the right research, but their choice is based on some version of weighing the upside potential and downside risk. We find options from those we trust, and try to get the best price for the cost of the resolution.
    - Preparation (know competition - SWOT exercise):
      _____
    - Next Step (they willing to requote on other's parameters):
      _____
    - Reminder (set reminder w/note):
      _____

Sales Tip: Buying Signals

Sales people should pick up on statements like; *"I like this," "I think that would be nice," "It would be great if," or "Do you have it in green?"* as the signals that mean, "I'm ready to purchase-help."

- *Buying Signal Story*: My wife was in the market for a new car. Though she started where she knew the GM of the dealership... I had asked her, "Please, let me do the negotiating—I do it for a living... It will be better if I am allowed to run this one..." **She found a car that she loved.** She kept giving me "big eyes" (while looking at the car). As if my lovely wife's subtle non-verbal style wasn't a clear enough signal... when we were walking away from the car (that she had decided she loved and could not live without), she adamantly said to me **in front of the sales rep**, "If this car isn't here tomorrow, I will hold you personally responsible."

  I turn to the sales rep and said, "I guess that's what we call a buying signal." He replied, "I think that is." He offered, "Do you want to come in and just buy it today— instead of having to come back tomorrow?" I said, "Yes, I do."

Buying signals say yes before the prospect does.

Tools used in Pipeline Activity:

In case you don't read any further, the most commonly used pipeline tool should be:

Computer Work: 3 min. Pre-Appointment Lookup

- Look them up on a Search Engine (personally and corporately)

- Look them up on a personal social network

- Look them up on a business social network or their website/blog

- Make record of anyone you know that is connected with them to bring up as possible trust building connectors

- Make note of personal occupational history of the person you're meeting (back to schools and groups)

Use the information you uncover as an introduction to their preferences. You never know, maybe they went to the 'beach vacation' because they're getting over divorce or death in the family. Don't assume; but pay attention

Computer Work: Share your Referrals.

If you don't have a website, send them to your Business' Social Media page or to your company's page on a directory. Your references are one of the main things that everyone is looking for (when they look you up on the web). Make it easy for them to find the endorsements they seek.

One step further: If you really appreciate the benefit of this (or any) computer work, buy a domain (they're cheap), and forward it to whatever page is to be highlighted. (i.e. recommendations for "Bob's Electrical Company" could be: endorsingelectricianbob.com).

5. Negotiation Preparation

Negotiation is a Conversation, which is just like a Game of Catch

No matter what the conversation is about, it's just a game of catch.

1. You throw out a thought like a ball (a statement or question).

2. They catch it (and listen).

3. They throw a response back to you, and the game of catch is on.

It doesn't always work perfect. There are times you throw a few balls, and they catch and arrange them on their desk. By the time you notice they're not throwing anything back, they have checked out and started to become overwhelmed. Like a fun game of catch, you need to stop throwing balls and politely ask them to throw one or two back before you can go on. That's how catch works.

Some people play catch wrong...

- *"Pelters"*: If you're someone who goes into a meeting and starts pelting balls/comments at everyone... there are people who are beat down enough, that they'll actually take it... and buy from you. You will (however) never experience long-term success, satisfaction in your business, or provide customer service because ***no one healthy in their interpersonal communication should enjoy being around you - it's like conversational bullying***.

- *"Hoarders"*: Hoarders take all the balls tossed at them, and hold onto them (and don't offer anything back). There may be some (Pelters) who will enjoy "interacting" with them (hoarders), but long-term success is virtually impossible because ***"hoarders" only take***.

Conversation is a game of catch—enjoy the game.

Use tools that simplify and streamline time invested:

- <u>Run an 3 Min Pre-Appointment Search on participants that RSVP for an event.</u> You will save hours per month in small-talk/lead-up chats - if you recognize someone that you researched, and lead the conversation. Websites and social networks offer powerful tools to research their backgrounds, current and previous colleagues, as well as activity preferences... use them.

- <u>Takes notes as you go:</u> It is often difficult to clearly remember the details from a conversation when it is time to follow up. Since the only thing you typically recall is what's written on their business card—take 30 seconds after each conversation to make notes on the back of their card.

- <u>Listen for whether or not you would enjoy doing business with them.</u> Quit sizing everyone up based on whether you can sell them what you offer. Start to consider if you would *enjoy* doing business with them, and then look for complementary opportunities. When you really listen to them, you will hear the buying signals given by a potential client.

- <u>Always have a prepared exit strategy:</u> When you're stuck, standing in front of a time waster—listen to their story, give a referral... and walk away. Again, a referral is a great escape. You don't have to refer a real person by passing on their contact information, home address, and children's names. Offer a business concept, a potential income channel, or an introduction to another networking group (that is full of time wasters like them)... almost anything that is articulate will work well—as long as "excuse me" is immediately followed by walking away.

Framing the Conversation

We create frames/assumptions/expectations around whatever social engagement we encounter. These are natural and good. A frame is the outline and boarder for the conversation we are in. We know what to assume, how to talk, what jokes are appropriate... we frame the conversation with our personal history.

When extraordinary or common events occur - we want to attribute meaning...

- o The meaning is determined (for the most part) by the "frame" or "framework" our memories of interpreted actions and recalled emotions are built around
- o When we change the frame, we altar how we perceive the circumstance (can be confusing for self/others)
- o When we change the frame after an occurrence - we change how we feel about our memory of the event
- o **Frames are best built before giving thought to an issue. Here are three to use:**

"What's the Solution" Frame:

- Many times what we give attention to - is what ends up happening (even if we don't want it to)... why?
  - o If you focus on and talk about the problem - the problem grows unless the focus is to find a solution
  - o Our focus and words give power to the object of our focus and words
  - o If we give our energy to the feeding on the problems (rather than a solution), our frame (boundaries) for future experience will be based on our mental history (starting with the problem)

"What I hear you saying is..." Frame:

- This is the marital counseling frame - greatest tool to combat miscommunication I've found
  - o There is no better way to make sure you are on the same page with your conversation partner - as completing the phrase, "What I hear you saying is..."

- Listen to their response (listen for the disconnects - not your priority)
- Find a single point of agreement/connection (which we call a baseline for the conversation)
- Use that point of common connection as a base & move forward with resolution
- *This is simply repeating back to them what you hear them saying & listening to what they tell you... believing that what they're giving as a response is just as aimed at clarity as your statements.*

"Let me ask a question" Frame:

- The reality of confusion in conversation is that one or more parties are either
  - Using different words to say the same thing (from different perspectives), or
  - In disagreement
- When disagreement (or lack of clarity) take place, the only response is to identify the point of confusion and work through it. Not everyone agrees, but everyone should be clear on what they are agreeing to.
  - We want to make sense of everything that happens to us - help your client achieve this

Sales Tip: Who goes 1st in Negotiation?

I've heard, "Never be the first one to give an offer during negotiation, because you may be too low."

There are circumstances in which this is true, but the one who goes first also sets the bar. There have been a number of times that I've allowed my prospect to give what they were expecting to spend (before I give the cost). It's almost always so low that I find myself struggling through the rest of the negotiation to pull it up to the point that I need to cover my costs.

A happy middle ground is found by getting their approximate budget up front... offer ranges (from $100-$200 or $500-$1,000 or whatever ranges fit your business). A film producer I worked with offers, "You can have 2 of the 3... Good, Cheap, or Fast—but you only get two of the three." **Set the bar.**

Mirroring to Build Rapport

What is Rapport? Regardless of the
perception or perspective with which you enter; *rapport is the process to establish trust, harmony and cooperation in a relationship.*

Everything in a sales appointment is built on Rapport. Rapport is (pretty much) everything a sales person does (and doesn't do) in order for the client to feel comfortable. Old school salesmen who "don't take no for an answer" are finished (thank God). The internet has removed the sales person's position as the resident expert. There is a (historically justified) reflexive distrust that is verified as soon as sales "stretches" the truth (lies). This natural distrust is hinged on the belief (from the client's perspective) that a sales person is only there for himself/herself (<u>which you are</u>); but the distrust is verified by a lack of rapport (which is the feeling on the client's end that you're full of it... only focused on making money).

The rule is to start with reality (what you know to be understood <u>by the client</u>), and go from there. If you recognize that you are perceived negatively (with distrust)—take it into account... and move forward (don't try to make them like you - it never works). All this adds together to require modern business people to possess real sales skills (to become the most trusted and liked option that their next client is looking for).

We all have our own map we follow. We only ever understand our own version of reality. It doesn't matter how hard we try to enhance or expand it (or how hard we try to enhance or expand other's perspectives). We never get outside of our translation of past experiences. We naturally think our opinion is right, or we would change our opinions... even though everyone's map is equally valid and rarely alike. Each reality map has been built through experience and the belief that we recorded circumstance accurately. **In business, there is a purpose for each meeting.** If you choose to push to be right in a negotiation; don't feel confused when you're not successful.

****
****

Nine Mirroring Techniques

****
****

Mirroring and Building Rapport Overview: *General types of mirroring techniques can be matched to your temperament and personality. We're only going to go through ten techniques.*

When it comes to mirroring it's important to understand that people like people who are <u>like</u> them. It sounds like double talk, but people prefer being around others who are similar to them.

|WARNING|

These are High Level Sales Tactics.

Use them cautiously.

One: The Crossover. This crosses over activities, but keep a synchronization of timing. Synchronize your speech with their breathing. Tap your pen with each point made by them. <u>This mirroring technique happens when your Actions Cross Over the other person's actions</u>. Your actions aren't the same, but your head will nod in line with their swiveling of their chair, or each time they end a sentence you tap your toe. It confirms that you are engaging them in your own way. People like to sense they are being followed, but not copied. All these mirroring techniques should be considered powerful and very effective, and always *keep in mind that they are most productive when they are **not recognized***.

- <u>Be patient</u>: If you're going to adjust your body position wait at least 20 to 30 seconds before you adjust. If you act like an actual mirror for their actions, it's creepy.

- <u>Be unintentional</u>: Don't have an accent to match theirs, but rather slips of phrase and tones. "Y'all" and "ain't" may be acceptable in a "Y'all" and "ain't" conversation, but only when the other person has similar communication pattern to yourself. Be Real.

- <u>Be comparable</u>: The size and scope of gestures should be matched to the size and scope of gestures of the other person, but to do the exact same gestures! It is insulting, and they will want to get away from you... because it looks like you're mimicking them (it looks desperate).

- <u>Be almost, but not quite</u>: If they are someone who crosses their hands in front of them (and looks like an evil genius from a James Bond movie); for you to do the same thing is silly. However, crossing your legs and leaning to the side is very acceptable mirror, because that allows you (when they uncross their hands to show an expression of openness) - to uncross your legs a couple of seconds later as a statement of openness. *It's also a solid tactic to uncross your legs/hands/whatever gesture is being used - before them... in an effort to encourage them to open up to the you (instead of being blocked off by having a barrier of their hands in front of them).*

If people catch on to what you're doing when you're mirroring... if you're too intentional... it becomes a complete turnoff so be aware that **rapport is a dance.** Don't step on their toes, but (even when you lead) follow the flow of the music of conversation. **Play the game of catch and enjoy the dance.**

* Note that most people do this naturally if they're truly engaged

Two: Physical Proximity. At times adjusting the focus and direction each party is facing (or the distance between you) can be used to adjust/alter the perception that positive progress is happening in this negotiation. There are times to sit across the desk discussing a proposal, and then (when the time is right), to move around and look at the same computer screen for a moment (to make a point) and move back to a comfortable distance after the moment of close proximity. Leaning in to create closeness can be something that creates an interest or intimidation. When you recognize that their interest has stepped in your direction... leaning up in your chair may look over zealous or (depending on how they are framing the conversation) it may subconsciously affirm their interest. If leaning in may appear desperate, another proximity move is to take off your glasses or set down (or pick up) your notepad to infer "we're getting serious now." Adjustment of physical proximity is natural when the negotiation is at an, "Okay. Let's figure out how this is going to happen" moment.

It's extremely important to pay attention to their response to your physical proximity move. At times it may cause a response of surprise and a pulling away or a nod of agreement. Offering, "Can I show you something on your computer" before looking at their computer screen will allow them to give you permission to be in close proximity for a time, but it's equally important how you step away and find an appropriate distance to move the conversation forward as soon as any non-verbal communication tells you that they'd like you back in your seat. Going from being next to each other (aiming at the same solution), and then across the table... may require you to lean in when you sit back down to keep a natural intimacy flow. Pay attention to the other person.

Gender specific/physical attraction attention is vital to take into consideration here:

Physical proximity can mean different things and can become a huge problem if both parties are not on the same page. It doesn't matter if there is or is not actual inappropriate proximity. The thought of crossing that line is an immediate loss (even when it doesn't seem like it should be). So... use proximity with caution and awareness.

Reality doesn't matter—just the client's perception of reality.

Three: Matching Language. The primary form of communication is verbal, and the complexity of hints passed back and forth is innumerable - yet crucial.

<u>We are all somewhere between Loquacious Bibliophiles to Slang Chatters (know your target):</u>

When dialoging with someone who loves to use big words, feel free to use big words, but *make sure you know what they mean.*

If a person uses complex vocabulary, but doesn't use the words correctly—understand they are making an effort to compensate for an assumed lack of education or knowledge (and want you to think they are more educated than they are) ... and that's OK. That type of person is easy to flatter and move in the direction you want.

In a conversation with someone who loves slang, feel free to use *YOUR* slang. You don't have to use the same slang they use. No matter what slang you use... <u>use it less frequently than they do</u>. Slang is a free flowing game, but everyone has a different indecipherable level with which they think slang is inappropriate in business. If you use their slang outside of your comfort zone—that can be a deadly serious mistake, especially when it's slang in which you are not fluent. There is also a growing risk (in our society) of using slang that is considered ethically or historically reserved for one group of people. Little will destroy rapport faster than using slang reserved for those who are inside that ethnicity or historically select group. If you're not one of them, don't pretend.

Warning on slang—it changes quickly. What you thought a word meant six months ago may not be what it means today. If my grandma said she felt gay and was going to have a fag... it would mean she felt happy and was going to have a cigarette. That is not the case today. Be yourself, people like that.

For Instance: Slang

If you're Caucasian speaking with an African-American and the African-American uses "Ebonics" ... your pretending that you use (or that you are somehow allowed to use) Ebonics is stupid for anyone who understands culture in America today. You may as well walk out of the room - you're done.

That being clear; I grew up in a Charismatic Pentecostal church and LOVE old school type "preaching." There is a rhythm and cadence to Ebonics that matches the cadence to preaching, and one of the rare times I get to use my "Pree-chaw" voice - is in those moments. If I'm naturally fluent in southern gospel emotionally impassioned banter... and enjoy that slang, I'm still very careful.

That is enough, as long as I am true to myself.

Four: Beliefs and Values. This could also be called a

politically correct form of mirroring. You don't have to believe the same to acknowledge and respect their views. I am personally a fan of the Denver Broncos football team. If I sit across from a huge Raiders fan, I can't tell them that I love the Raiders, because it's wrong (and a mortal sin as a Broncos fan). I can, however, transition and begin to talk about how great football is, and mention a common rival (like the Chiefs).

This may be one of the most dangerous mirroring techniques to use in our society, so be careful.

You can tell a personal story that reflects similar beliefs and values (thinking that you're on the same page), but beliefs and values are sticky and messy when you get it wrong (even a little piece of it). The fact that you think you are on the same side (of a particular divide) doesn't mean *they think* you are on the same side. There are subtle distinctions people make for who is and is not on their side, and you may not be aware of what they see as the points of division. These details of social distinctive divides are confusing, rarely completely logical, and almost always tied to deep seeded emotional triggers (when they're offended).

Five: Voice Inflection. This includes; pitch, volume, pause, or any number of 'tells' that hint vocally... to the inflection being communicated.

- Are their statements made at a steady consistent pace typically or never? (did it change)

- Are they talking really fast because they can think fast or because they're nervous?

- Is there a change between statements and questions? What change?

- Do they speak slow and with methodical precision, or is their conversation slow (as if they're searching for an answer)?

If they are someone who speaks slow and intentional - and you're a fast talker; you're seen as someone who is not going to take the time to get to know them (or what they want and need) ... thus; you will never have rapport with them - just because you didn't mirror their voice inflection.

Pauses are VITAL! The length and comfort with which pauses are used is an important part of voice inflection. People either appreciate pauses or they are afraid of them. If you enjoy elongated pauses, and you're across from one who is nervous—it may make you feel like you are in control... but you appear to be searching or just uncomfortable to the communicator who never pauses.

Tangents can be bonding or a waste of their time. Do they get straight to the point or give personal stories to verify the end result (and get there eventually)?

1. If they are tangent people and you're direct and to the point, rapport will be lost because you're not letting them make the

decision on their terms. If they are people that weigh their options making decisions (by taking the circular route), your direct route (though it may be the most precise) won't give them the chance to take the path they are comfortable with. It will often feel like an intense and selfish interrogation to the circular thinker. If this is what you want (because you don't want this type of client or want to get a decision and move on) that is an acceptable filtering process, but if you need the business... sometimes you need to follow the directions they give you.

2. If they are straight forward and you get off topic, you lose. You are to mirror them. They shouldn't recognize that you're doing anything of the sort - they should only feel like you are really understanding what they are trying to communicate (rapport).

Six: Pacing and Leading. After you've mirrored the person for a while, but progress seems to have lulled—there is a time and place in the sales cycle to create movement.

Pacing and leading conversation can be done through altering your breathing, or pace of communication; with any of these other mirroring tools of conversations. It is possible to direct the other person to magnetically draw them to your conversational aims. This can be used to either calm them down, to excite them, to draw them in toward you, or push them away—at the appropriate time.

As with any type of leading, the only prerequisite is to be *at least one step ahead* of those you lead. Advanced mirroring tools (like this) allow you to adjust the pace of the conversation in order to lead it somewhere. Don't try to lead without a clear direction. If you think you lead and no one follows... you're just taking a walk (and that walk in negotiation is out the door).

<u>Seven:</u> Emotional Connection. Emotion is most

commonly communicated with the eyes and skin on the face. There are (of course) other physical, verbal, and non-verbal cues, but the face and eyes can usually tell it all.

The easiest reads of emotions are found in the squinting and widening of the eyes. Any toddler understands this, but the reason for pointing it out here is: **if you don't look them in the eye—you can't see what any toddler could read.**

Justify emotion by matching pace, volume, and even speed or scope of facial contortions. Even though we buy based (at least partially) on feelings, we don't know how each other is actually feeling (we just get the clues). If you start to track them (emotionally) you have the chance to uncover points of need or concern that may not come out otherwise. ***This requires establishing a baseline for their emotional state to recognize variations brought on by emotions felt.***

At times; be willing to adjust your course after matching emotion. You're there to do business and not get a hug. An emotional point of connection can be powerful, but the ability to redirect back to the deal at hand is masterful. Change the topic back to the last point they connected with you on a business level (checkpoint), and wrap it up.

Rule of Thumb <u>Emotions control or are controlled</u>

If you're emotionally healthy, it's a powerful thing to mirror emotionally; but if you're someone that has trouble controlling your emotions (anger, excitement, or lust), don't play here.

- *If you're showing concern; a slight eye squint while looking down and then look back at them as you allow your squint to relax communicates empathy.*

- *To follow the same process (but not relax your face as you look at them) will communicate confusion (due to past hurts or whatever is inside that's distracting you).*

People make purchases on emotion—so you need to use this wisely (or not at all). There is no recovery from an emotional offense.

Eight: Breaking Rapport. This is a very important piece of mirroring!

Building rapport isn't limited to always building rapport, but also breaking it (because you need a quick reset). You're at the table for your purpose; whether you're buying or selling.

Everyone has their own ways of doing this... Looking at your watch... Tilting your head... Whatever you do... begin to do it on purpose (and watch for what others do as well as their response to your breaking rapport mechanism).

Learning to break rapport with grace and style can also make uncomfortable circumstances much, much simpler. You don't need to worry about, "I was stuck in a conversation" again. When you need to be done, be done. You can pick up the conversation later.

Quick tip: Have a phrase. "Thoroughly enjoyed meeting you, but I need to go [FILL_IN_THE_BLANK]. Excuse me" and walk off. It's okay. That response is politer than a real "talker" is used to.

Game: How people say, "Enough"

It is incredibly entertaining to begin to record how your boss and friends break rapport. Everyone has their own process they use (usually without recognition).

Watch them at an event (or any conversation). When they're done with a conversation, each of us will typically try to leave (break rapport). As you recognize the tool they use to move on, make note of it, but don't mention it (people get weird about being predictable).

The next time you see them use it, be a help to them and provide a way out—you'll be their best friend (even if they don't say it).

Nine: Physical Lead.

Humans have a habit of mimicking what they are looking at. This is done without intent, but... everyone does it. Physical leads are the most obvious (and thus the most conspicuous) type of mirroring. Due to this obvious nature, there is a large risk of being exposed during this type of mirroring (if you're not careful). No one likes to be manipulated.

Example: Head nodding = yes (even if they're verbalizing no). If you are nodding your head yes it makes them begin to nod their head yes, and makes it difficult to say the word no.

Recognize what physical reactions you have to the different internal decisions that you make. You are the safest control for testing these tools, because you know what you're actually feeling (use a mirror). Begin to (slightly) make those physical actions as you want your prospect to make the same internal decisions—physically lead them to the decision.

For Instance: Gender and Sex and Physical Proximity?

When I was in corporate sales, I went on a cold call where the front desk girl (probably 22 years old) was standing with five or six mixed gendered coworkers showing off a new tattoo she had (on her chest). It was in clear sight of everyone and was the only office conversation taking place.

I walked in to cold call and since everyone was talking about it (joined the conversation to create rapport). I offered a complement with, "That's a great tattoo. I really like it."

She called my general manager and told him how inappropriate I was and that I was, "talking about her boobs."

Thankfully, the general manager knew me well and laughed as he came to me (explaining the message he had received from this girl).

Lesson Learned.

Ten: Sensory based words.

The best mirroring technique has definitely been saved for last in this list **(even though it's been addressed before - this stuff really works).**

One of the most powerful tools in the behavioral sales and marketing arsenal is the ability to match sensory specific words to internal language. If we process our world through one specific sensory type - we feel like we connect with people who use those same sensory words.

- This not only gives you an immediate "on the same page" status, but it also exposes the internal processing preferences of your prospect "soon to be" client.

- If you pay attention, everyone you speak with will tell you what their primary and secondary sensory input channels are; and this exposes the words they use to justify their decisions.

Samples of sensory responses that say the same thing:

- "I see what you mean."

- I hear what you're talking about."

- "I'm feel like we're on the same page."

- "I think this makes sense."

If you use their sensory specific words in your response... you will be speaking the same language (and put yourself in a position of success).

Game Using Tells and Mirroring

A thoroughly enjoyable exercise is to **pick one of these techniques for the next week**, and give attention to how it is used by you (and then by others). Speak in the first, second and third person perspectives, and focus on how people use mirroring. Figure out how people do rapport. Look for which sensory types prefer which conversational perspectives. You'll be surprised how enjoyable it is when you can read people around you... and how well you will get to know yourself in pursuit of understanding others.

Word from experience; be careful teaching these to your children.

- *My oldest daughter (probably 7-8 years old) attended a meeting with me, and when we were done she turned to me and she said, "Daddy, I think he's lying." Flabbergasted at this bold statement I asked why. She said, "Because where he was looking every time he answered your questions. Every time he answered he would look up and to my left - that means he's making it up... right?"*

We had previously talked about eye direction and what it means. **She may have been right, but it was not a tool she had the ability to handle at the time, because it's not a rule, but a typical pattern... like most these techniques.**

Mirroring is not an infallible science.

These are all guides and tools to bring an apparent sense of comfort to your conversation. Your actions and words are able to smooth the way to accomplish your desired end. Through knowledge of who you're sitting across from (and what state of mind they're in) you can increase your potential of success and enjoyment.

The tools work so, become good at them.

Resetting the conversation

Do you want to be Right or Happy?

When I was a young married man, there was an "old guy" in our church who befriended me (for some reason), and I gladly considered Ray a close friend of mine.

My wife and I arrived early for church band practice one Sunday; and we were obviously fighting on the drive (I lead the band and my bride played violin). As I would give instructions; she would glare at me as if to say, "Make me." For some reason I felt that arguing back was right... because I was the "leader." Our little band in a little church felt so important in that circumstance. She needed to follow my instructions - so that we would play everything just right. We were clearly bickering while the rest of the band watched.

Ray (always showing up early) pulled me aside after the practice, put his arm around me, and in a grandfatherly way said, *"Dan, I've been married for decades and the one thing I've learned through years of marriage is that **you have the opportunity to be right or be happy**... but you get to make the choice."*

Ray was right that the best choice was to be happy.

Sometimes we all get caught in a conversation we shouldn't be in and need a reset.

****
****

Every reset starts with the Baseline:

Negotiations should always start with a common point (or baseline). This is called an Upfront Contract, or Working Agreement... but basically is the foundation from which the rest of the conversation is built.

During negotiation we recognize there is something blocking progress (we can't see eye to eye), but our natural and self-preserving response is to push against each other to make sure "I" am taken care of. This is why sales (many times) feels like you're butting heads, because you are.

Neither party is really listening to each other because both are looking for the next opening to get their version of the truth into the other person; it's like two people in a sword fight, but standing too far apart for their swords to even touch. Both feel like they're doing a great job, but nothing is actually happening.

When it's time to use a Baseline Reset:

- People on both sides of a negotiation start to stare at the other side of the table, and search for any morsel that can be applied or beneficial to "my point"

- We forget that we're in a discussion. The room is full of multiple narcissistic monologues (with sections of silence that are used to say the same thing with different words)

- Every person, place, and thing you've encountered that might be associated with the negotiation becomes a prop for either of you to make/win your point

- Instead of listening, you are trying to figure a hole in your fellow negotiator's thinking to wedge your thoughts into

Reality check: the other person has a legitimate (and usually intelligent) reason for why they're thinking what they're thinking. Chances have it—they're trying to figure out the gap in your perspective that you have obviously overlooked or you would see/hear/feel/think in the same way they do (they think it is their job to expose this gap to you).

As you see this cycle beginning (or catch that you've fallen into this rut); **stop and go back to the baseline**, from which you began.

Global Issue Situational Narcissism?

There's a new psychological disorder that's become common and recognized as "situational narcissism." *Celebrities often have this. If I live long enough (with every person around me telling me that I do nothing wrong), I'll start to believe that I'm always right... and I'll start to believe them. It is seductive to close your eyes to all views except your own, and believe everyone else's knowledge and belief reasoning to be inferior my own – it's just gross.*

The lack of personal contact facilitated by the web is making this disorder available to everyone... even common.

Children and adults alike are able to express opinions and make comments on friends, foes, and social problems without being responsible for their words (face to face). An insulation of perspective can kill while not having to watch our victims die. *Not good.*

Write down Checkpoints along the way

The Checkpoint Frame is an extension of The Baseline Frame. If the only option (after an hour of talking) is to go back to the initial baseline of the conversation... it's like admitting that everyone's time has been wasted (up to that point).

As a good business person: this is a failure on your part. If you find yourself locked in a negotiation and neither party seems to be able to find a next step:

- Go back to the last point you felt or thought that you connected, and restate the point of agreement as a checkpoint.
- Confirm the points you agree and restart from there.

Checkpoints function like points on a spiral. Each time you pass that point, another checkpoint is created - and agreement is built. As you get closer to the center (the desired point of negotiated compromise) ... the checkpoints grow closer together and agreement is found.

Creating checkpoints that are closer together is a sign that the negotiation cycle is being reduced to the point of resolution and decision.

- Find a common point that you agree on to begin (baseline).
- Establish the agreed upon factors for decision during the negotiation (checkpoints).
- Establish all factors that you agree on (at each of the checkpoints) building on the baseline.

- o   If there are many issues articulated, list them in order of priority.

Many points of negotiation are realized to be peripheral upon review of the factors in the final decision. Unless the primary points of pain are established (baseline), you will find yourself negotiating totally different issues than the prospect (even though you are using the same words). You will assume you're "almost there," but won't even have a connection at the baseline point of pain that needs to be resolved. You will plan on getting a big paycheck in 30 days, and not have a clue that the client is purchasing a completely different product than what you are presenting (likely from some other sales rep or business owner) ... who will have a great payday, take *their* spouse on a nice vacation, and thank you... because *they* resolved the real baseline issue and firmed up the checkpoints along the way.

Rephrasing for Clarity with "What I hear you saying is"

This is the second time that this question is referenced here, but it's important. This wonderfully powerful tool not only helps business, but every other area of life that deals with people communicating ...*especially when emotions get in the way.* We're going through it twice to make sure it sticks.

Steps to use this tool:

1.   Listen to what they have to say—actively.

2.   Say, "Now what I hear you saying is," followed by a re-statement of what you think they are communicating— **in your own words**.

3.   If they jump in (at any point) to correct your rephrasing;

- o   wait for them to finish

- o start over once you listen to how they adjusted your rephrasing.
4. Confirming that what you have said sums up their position; move on to continue to build checkpoints upon this base.

For Instance: Why politics are so polarized?

Most political (or any heated) arguments are based on two things:

1. We are arguing to change the other person's mind, because we assume they just don't know what we do. We don't listen (and seek first to understand), because they aren't listening to us.

2. We don't reason through what is being said, because we're afraid they will win - and that's worse than anything.

This is an ugly part of our system of government, but carries an obvious application that applies to business. *They may disagree with almost all your points, but a baseline reset in negotiation is like a safety net—if you're willing to not assume they're stupid (just because they don't agree with you), you have the ability to listen, understand, and use wisdom to find a solution.*

KEY #1 TO MOVING FORWARD: Accept that they aren't as crazy as you think they are. Be okay with the fact that they aren't right (in your eyes), but that doesn't mean they have to change... It's a start to finding the common ground. Compromise isn't a negative characteristic, it's a pattern of selecting the details of a priority that aren't vital on both sides, selecting the singular priority being addressed, and creating the framework around which the solution is mapped out.

KEY #2 TO MOVING FORWARD: The points that are important to the final decision are **the points that are vital to the final decision-maker signing off on the deal.** Know your target.

Remember... Be Polite

If there is one thing that the shrinking world of this digital revolution has exposed... you don't know the details inside of another person. They may be another religion, sexual identity, etc - and a wrong word can explode... simply due to your... being you. Your ignorance of their perspective doesn't mean you have to be stupid and make mistakes...

Don't be stupid; be polite.

13 The Rules of digital communication:

1. Be Yourself
2. You're talking to people – not computers
3. What you type is who you are
4. Be Accurate and Excellent (Spelling & Grammar errors can disqualify you)
5. Make others feel important, with sincerity
6. Avoid typing in all capital letters (unless you're yelling... and why would you yell?)
7. Avoid racy humor & profanity
8. Wait to reply until you're no longer angry
9. Give unsolicited endorsements. Distribute them.
10. Never criticize, condemn, or complain
11. Be genuinely interested in other people, talk in terms of other's interests
12. Act happy and have fun, make them want to engage
13. Listen, encourage others to talk about themselves

6. Analyze and Adjust (weekly-monthly)

Quit wishing things will change without changing your action.
No change (or lack of change) affects only you.

With any change, you need to assess:

Who will be affected by this taking place?

_____

Will this campaign's success affect only a part of my life or encompass all areas?

_____

Are there pieces that it cannot affect?

_____

If it is work based, will it also have an effect on what is personal? If it's personal, can I hide it from work?

_____

When do you want this outcome to be the only thing you're focusing on?

_____

Consider the context, or plan on sabotage!

Set up an Ongoing Assessment of your Pipeline

After using scripts for a period of time it is a common tendency to "adjust" and "improvise" to the point that we are giving useless or counter-productive additions to the script/outline. Review the Scripts, Quotas, Pipeline, etc. on a scheduled basis. Place an event on your calendar (must have a reminder) to repeat this process and make sure you're still being efficient and excellent in your system and communication.

Rule of Thumb - Weakest link

A chain is a series of links that are interconnected (just like a marketing and sales campaign cycle). It is nothing more than a series of links, and it only takes one of them to release the tension (that it is experiencing) ... for the purpose of the chain to be lost.

If you are changing anything, you're creating a new chain (of events), and in effect creating a new campaign plan. Your daily life is where all these pieces fit into action. If there is one point that will weaken and release due to tension—your entire chain will "break."

A chain is only as strong as its weakest link... oh, you've heard this before... why are you still surprised when this law goes into effect?

7 ...Finally; Get a Mentor

Modeling minimizes the necessary timeline between inability and proficiency (especially within marketing and sales). If the structure used by an expert is broken down into accomplishable steps, it is (in an over-simplified manner), a matter of scheduling those steps into your daily life. **The statement, "What one man or woman can do another can do," is absolutely true.**

If you desire abilities not currently in your skillset, you have one of two options:

1. Personally experience all the pitfalls and trials involved in the process of developing expertise.

2. Revisit the master-apprentice relationship, and have someone better at it help you.

Keep in mind that someone being model worthy in one area of their life doesn't mean they should be followed in every area. The goal is not to become the other person, but to learn to mimic the actions and internal processes that enable them to function and behave in a way that you currently cannot.

Global Issue: Where did the mentors go?

The biggest hurdle to good modeling (in our culture) is pride. The student speaks up to the teacher and either gives an excuse for the student to not do it the same way, or a correction of the teacher... explaining how the teacher is off.

We seem to have celebrated ingenuity to the point that we have to relearn the basics of life every generation.

We have lost the concept of master in our culture. Someone who is trusted implicitly. *It's apparent that most people who are put in positions of authority prove that they should not be trusted.*

If Warren Buffett asked to show you how to invest, you would drop everything and listen. There are specialists everywhere—not all of them are a celebrity.

Go look for Insight Brokers.

Broad overview of the Process:

1. Finding someone that is capable of what you are not.

2. Understand the acting and thinking patterns that expert uses.

3. Break down the expert's actions and habits into small enough steps to follow them.

In the movie *The Matrix*, one could plug their brain into a computer and open their eyes after a few seconds and say with certainty, "I know Kung Fu" (pretty cool). Even though it takes a little more time than a few fluttering blinks—that is how modeling works, *through time*.

Modeling Process:

First, determine the desired ability. Without a target selected, there is a solid chance that we will merely envy another person's lifestyle (and experience no personal benefit). We're modeling what takes place in a certain area of expertise <u>in</u> or <u>through</u> the mentor.

Second, identify someone to be your example/model. Depending on the ability and proximity, it may be a good idea to get permission from them. Watch them, pay attention, confirm that they're better at the skill/ability you want to acquire, and identify the recognized examples for why you will use them as your model.

The purpose is to enable an ability (like ability to close a sale on the first call or have the best customer retention) ... NOT mimicking unrelated characteristics (which is dangerous and creepy) ...and worst of all counterproductive.

Third, make note of applicable behaviors, states and actions.

This is not just tracking what they say, but how they say it. If you have not received permission to use them as your subject and start to keep a written journal... it's a good idea to communicate to someone else that you're using them (so you don't get a restraining order against you).

This is not only obvious and large gestures, but micro-movements that are used in between what is easily seen. Track the eye movements before and after questions, when they squint, when they take off their glasses, variations of breath and how deep each takes place. Then, begin to test out the mentor's actions and behaviors yourself.

Recognize and engage in the same micro-movements with *how they say what they say*. Begin to sort which pieces of modeling are necessary for you to create a new skillset, and which are not related to the ability—merely create the personal habits you consider beneficial to your marketing and sales campaign to be successful.

Fourth, remove the pieces that don't affect performance.

Your goal is not to become the person, but to model and mirror their experience. Record the pieces of action and behavior that are *not consistent with who you are*. Nothing is more annoying (and dangerous) than someone who mimics without an understanding of self. Remove what's not beneficial, don't remove things just because they feel unnatural. Everything is unnatural until you've done it a few times.

Fifth, clearly define the mindset and actions required to produce the desired results.

Personally, I

find that writing these specifics down in my task list or notebook delivers the quickest and most productive results. This allows me to keep these actions and thought patters in front of me (and review them at will). If there's something I want to engage (that's going to involve a lengthy process), write them in a location that is accessible but not intrusive, because if you add items to your task list that aren't going to be completed for a year—your task list loses its value.

Sixth, list the points you are incompetent and create a schedule for acquiring competency.

I realize that this seems like it should be earlier in the process of modeling; but it is difficult to admit incompetence, and we usually don't know what we're actually incompetent at until we've been trying to fix it for a little bit. We have a tendency to either say, "I got it down," or, "I can't do it." Not everyone can be the best, and no one can acquire every ability; but any specific competency is available through focused intentional application (and a little help from someone who knows how to do it).

Seventh, create reminders to insure the new pattern doesn't get lost or dropped.

It's usually a lot more fun to start a project (and dream of the benefits to be experienced upon completion) rather than grinding out a new pattern of activity. As is the case with any purposeful endeavor—don't start if you don't have the fortitude to finish. If you do have the guts to complete a change in yourself that makes you more of who you want to be... give yourself reminders to make sure life doesn't get in the way.

<u>For Instance: They were friends growing up...</u>

Have you ever noticed the number of great athletes and thinkers that (after they are recognized for their greatness) reveal that they been old friends with others who have achieved the same level of greatness? Two of the top professional athletes are playing in the finals and during the game the TV commentator points out they played together in kid's leagues growing up. Multiple scientists or writers are respected for completely different areas of expertise; but in review of history, we see that they were friends and spent copious amounts of time together at the pub.

- **There are ways of thinking and living that make us great (and/or completely handicap our endeavors).**

- **Great people are great (many times) because they shared the same tools and avoided the same pits as those around them.**

A pitfall a mentor of mine taught me:

My dad's favorite saying when I was growing up was, ***"If a job has once begun, never leave it till it's done. Be the labor great or small, do it well or not at all."*** I hated it. I cringed each time I heard the opening six words. Don't tell my dad this, but I'm grateful for annoying phrases being so consistently beat into my thinking… that I can't stop hearing them over and over every time I want to quit. My dad knows how to finish. Thanks dad for mentoring that truth into my actions, because it still doesn't feel natural… I just know it's good truth.

NOTES:

NOTES:

NOTES:

NOTES:

NOTES:

NOTES:

NOTES:

NOTES:

NOTES: